MW01243534

"Tattered Hues"

In case anyone ever doubts,
A Dirty Kid, the homeless,
I gotta SHOUT!

It's never been about a book,
Festered jewels,
a pleather hook.

It's always been
about you,
Tattered,
Broken ...
Love-filled Hues

~Poppa Chuck~

The When Sidewalks Smile Project is a 501(c)3 nonprofit project dedicated to raising awareness that every individual in the street community is a person longing to be seen and heard. A human with a beautiful heart, longing to have purpose and be of value to this world, just like we all do.

In honor of every heart in the street community who has touched Poppa Chuck's heart and cared for him (which are far too many to count), The When Sidewalks Smile Project is making a gift to the Portland Rescue Mission, Transition Projects, and other homeless resources with a portion of the proceeds from this book. The remaining funds are directed back to The When Sidewalks Smiles Project for future publications and endeavors. The second edition is scheduled to be available by Spring 2022.

To learn more; go to whensidewalkssmile.org.

Printed in the U.S.A.

First printing January 2022

The "When Sidewalks Smile" Project, NPO
Portland, Oregon 97205

whensidewalkssmile.org

https://www.facebook.com/search/top?q=when%20sidewalks%20smile

Foreword

"Come, you who are blessed by my [Father], inherit the Kingdom prepared for you from the foundation of the world. For I was hungry and you gave me food, I was thirsty and you gave me drink, I was a stranger and you welcomed me, I was naked and you clothed me, I was sick and you visited me, I was in prison and you came to me."

Then the Just [those without prejudice or partiality] will answer him, saying, "Lord, when did we see you hungry and feed you, or thirsty and give you drink? And when did we see you a stranger and welcome you, or naked and clothe you? And when did we see you sick or in prison and visit you?"

And the King will answer them, "Truly, I say to you, as you did it to one of the least of [these], you did it to me."

~Yeshua of Nasrath

Every once in a while, on this journey we call 'Life,' one encounters a person who leaves such a deep impression on your heart that you absolutely know you are meant to be life-companions. Aligned in heart and commitment to serve others; specific 'others.'

For Joseph and me, that encounter was with Chuck Walker (aka Poppa Chuck). After learning about the images my husband, Joseph Paulicivic, was taking of a group of 'home-free' nomads, affectionately called, *Dirty Kids,* Chuck decided to check us out.

Turns out, we were on a very similar path; called by Love to raise awareness to the general public about this community within the homeless population, as well as to raise the self-image and value among the *Dirty Kids...one Kid at a time.*

One might expect to find someone serving food or offering warm clothing to those less fortunate than them as an act of kindness. But we found Chuck on the streets of Portland, Oregon, giving so much more to the outcasts, the rejected, the abandoned, the devalued, the dirty, the addicts, the weary, the cold, and the sick. Chuck was giving them his life; his time, his resources, his friendship, his compassion.

There is a sea of people representing one religious affiliation or another 'giving' to the homeless. But when you look just below the 'gift' (a blanket or food), you find another agenda; to 'save' them.

People don't need to be saved; people need love.

The *Dirty Kids* can sniff out an agenda a mile away, and they react strongly to agendas, regardless of whether it's a religious agenda or another personal agenda.

Joseph and I learned this from our own experience with the *Dirty Kids* the previous several years of sitting with them and listening to their stories. What was clear from the very first encounter with Chuck on the streets of Portland, Oregon, was this man's only agenda was to love these people, to make certain, beyond a shadow of a doubt, that they would know that he was interested in them as human beings; human beings with a story, who longed to be seen and heard, just like everyone longs for. Human beings who also longed to have a purpose and be of value to this world, just like all of us do.

And so, Poppa Chuck did just that! He offered his resources, his time, his heart, and even his own wounds to be a vessel of Love, to love the unloved, as well as to receive the love he so desperately needed to become a *healed*-healer.

In the pages of this memoir, you will read of the most unlikely heroes; the outcasts and outlaws, the addicts and abused, the wounded warriors coming to the rescue of a stranger in need as they danced together in the single act of giving and receiving; giving and receiving value, love, dignity, strength, vulnerability, companionship, and hope.

Foreword

Joseph and I are now seven years into our experience with the *Dirty Kids*. Joseph has gathered and shared over 200 images with this community. As a result of these images, we have had the great pleasure of joining our hearts and our mission with several other people who have committed their lives to serving the *Dirty Kids* community. It takes a very special person with a very special grace to do this work. Chuck is that man. You truly can't perform or pretend your way through a ministry like this. Everything one needs to be sustained on this path is a Divine gift of Love. This memoir is an invitation into the heart of God [Love] through the experience of the lives presented on these pages.

If you have never spent time with a stranger in this way, I promise your life will be changed as a result of reading these stories. Here you will meet some beautiful human beings doing extraordinary acts of kindness with very few resources in some of the darkest places a person can find themselves.

Get ready to have your eyes opened, and your heart expanded! You will never see a homeless person the same again.

In Service to *Love,*
Denise Darlene-Paulicivic
(Author of *"Real Passion Revolution"*)

Joseph Paulicivic III
(Photographer/Author of
"Dirty Kids: Word on the Street")

This book is lovingly dedicated to:

Merab & Lindsey

Evander, Sophia & Lilah

"Buster" & "Z"

Zephyrus

Nathaniel & Savannah

Dubhlainn

Adalyn

...And all the children of those not lost,
but intimately found
on the streets and sidewalks,
where love stuck out
like a sore Dirty Kid's thumb...

When
Sidewalks
Smile

An Old Guy's Unexpected and Beautiful Journey into the Hearts of the Homeless

Charles Walker Jr aka Poppa Chuck

Foreword ~ Denise Darlene-Paulicivic

Table of Contents

Table of Contents

A Special Thank You

To *Providence Portland Medical Center*, doctors, nurses, and staff of the 4th floor for their exemplary care in the spring of 2018. Without your encouraging and nurturing hearts and that of Love, I would not be able to see to type these words and share the beauty I've found in the hearts of our street communities.

To my daughters, Merab Elizabeth and Lindsey Ruth (the Niz & the Bub), thank you for always believing in me when I could not. Your vision that something this extravagant would be a part of my journey has finally come to fruition. You are the brightest Lovelights of my life. Without the hope that is you, I probably would have left this Earth long ago.

To my mother, Esther Maxine, thank you for being my rock and for all of your patience and love throughout my life!

To Joseph and Denise Paulicivic, thank you for all of your extravagant love, support, and sharing this beautiful walk of love with me.

To the Well Community Church for your prayers and for loving me back to sight.

To David Botts (my street buddy and "pastor"), for reminding me that I have a loving heart, to live my faith, and for being my pastor when no one else could. Please know you have fulfilled your destiny by speaking Love's truths into the heart of this old guy. For, when I was in need, you gave to me out of the goodness of your heart; food, drink, friendship, brotherhood, laughter, and tears. I am forever grateful for our friendship and for the bond which ties us together, the bond that is purely and distinctly… Love.

To Lindsey LeGore, for being my first *amazing* editor, keeping me on track, nurturing, and gently guiding me into believing in this project (and myself).

To my sister Carole Estherchild (amazing editor #2), thank you for being so very patient with me, putting up with my stubbornness, and taking on my very challenging writing style.

To Lori Banks for simply always being there, nurturing and loving me unconditionally.

A huge shout out to Marsha Fulton of MyPurplePen, Proofreading Editor Extraordinaire! You polished the manuscript to perfection and actually made me fall in love with it!

To Sidewalk and every heart in the Dirty Kid and Street Communities, thank you for being a light in the darkness. Your support, participation, and belief in this project kept me going. But more importantly, thank you for the love, support, and friendship you've given this old guy over the years. I'll never be the same. Unconditional Love is the journey. Thank you for living the journey. Without each of you, there would be no book and rarely a moment, *"When Sidewalks Smile."*

And most of all, a shout out to Love for taking me on this journey; impossible it would be …*without You!*

Preface

The sidewalks of my world, for the most part, have often been my only friend, my safe place. Where I hung my head, staring only at the pavement as I walked to and from school as a small boy. It was like I walked on the eggshells of scorn through each day, avoiding the eyes that judged me, the frowning with a shaming glance, the eyes with a knowing look of disgust; inflicting judgments, paralyzing, choking me.

I was different from the other boys in grade school and certainly made very aware of that by my peers. Most often (even at home with my family), I felt unwanted, ashamed, alone, and scared. I was an outcast.

Not realizing it as a child and teen, I was in a dark relationship with the sidewalks; pain, shame, and gloom walked hand in hand with me. I feared men; I feared judgment, even the speculation that I was different. Adults called me melancholy; it made me feel damaged and useless.

I once believed that depression was one of my greatest enemies. It crippled me many times throughout my life, most likely back to when I was in my mother's womb. Yet, it took the debilitating depths of Post-Traumatic Stress, Severe Depression, and anxiety disorders to provide Love (my epithet for Creator, the Universe, God, etc.) with the tools necessary to lead me on a challenging but enlightening journey.

I made the best of life as I grew into adulthood. Even though I never felt like I fit in, I did try. I started working when I was 16, entering a Work Release program in High School, minimizing the amount of time I spent at school, which was a relief to me. I made good friends at work, mostly with women. I still felt shunned by men. I tried going to college after graduating from High School. The anxiety disorder (I didn't know what it was back then) kept me on edge in all my classes. Whenever I took tests, my brain shut down. I failed all of my classes. I was in a constant state of melancholy.

At the age of 21, in 1977, it was like a light switch was flipped on. I had a spiritual awakening, got married, started a family, and made friends with the guys at work. Life was perfect. Until four years into our marriage, the depression, anxiety, and fear reared their ugly head once again. I began to struggle with my sexuality as well. It was a three-year living nightmare! My wife and I separated seven years into our marriage, then amicably divorced a year later. I hated myself. The men at work began making fun of me, calling me a faggot and homo. It was like being in grade school all over again. But far worse! I realized my hometown was not a safe place for me. The oppression was insane! Depression, anxiety, self-loathing, and fear gripped me so hard I took to self-medicating, first on cocaine, then on methamphetamine. Within three years, I was diagnosed with HIV.

After those three years of pure hell and nonsensical behavior, I quit meth, got a job at Oregon Health Sciences University in Portland, Oregon, and started a journey of self-acceptance, even starting to love myself. I worked at OHSU for ten years. It was an amazing experience with my bosses working hard to build my self-confidence and self-worth. They actually believed in me. I learned a great deal about serving all types of people with harsh disabilities and life-threatening illnesses. I loved every position I held at OHSU, my coworkers, and all of the patients. Many of the patients were homeless and drug users. I learned to look past that. Anxiety and depression were in remission. Oppression had been replaced with freedom and a renewed love for life. No one ever batted an eye at the fact that I was HIV positive.

Then life happened again. After nine years of employment at OHSU, it became a highly stressful environment. Anxiety took hold once again. The staff joked about putting antidepressants in the water system. My partner and I split up after five years together. I dove headfirst into a new relationship which was not only unhealthy, but it was an unhealthy relationship as well. A few months thereafter, I began to self-medicate. I left my job and continued to use for six months. I then ended the relationship with meth and with my partner, regained my composure and self-worth, then ventured on to another wonderful employer, Fanno Creek Clinic.

Relapses and recovery were to become a common theme in my life. But still, I pressed on fighting the feelings that I didn't fit in, was an outcast, and was unwanted. I was diagnosed with Clinical Depression in 2001.

Through my experiences working in the medical field, I became somewhat comfortable with serving the neglected outcasts of our society. In 2014, working as a Peer Support Specialist with homeless men, I was blessed to attend training seminars by Social Justice Advocates like Donna Beegle (one of my social justice *heroes*). While attending her seminars, I came to realize that I feared people living on the streets, in alleyways, and under bridges. I was taught to fear them while growing up; by my family, peers, and society as a whole. We lived in a small, blue-collar, white-bread town. We truly didn't know any better. Loathing the unfortunates was the socially 'acceptable' worldview back in the day.

Yet, that revelation wasn't enough. Love desired to take me on an intimate journey, to see into the hearts of the outcasts firsthand. Nor was it enough for me to see the extent of judgment my own heart held towards them *and* others in my small world. I realized I judged everyone and everything in some way. Love needed to take me on an 'insiders' journey, where everything I thought I was and everything I thought to be truth (actually the unripened fruit of truth) came into question. Ironically, this journey would lead me into an even deeper state of despair than I'd ever known. I was soon to become *one* ... with the darkness.

The darkness of depression and anxiety led me to self-medicate, yet once again after six years at FCC. I had given up on myself and life. I was hopeless, briefly ending up on the streets, homeless and drug-addicted. There, my very small and ignorance-challenged world was torn wide open as I began meeting and developing unlikely and unexpected friendships with notorious, cunning, and charismatic yet endearing characters. They all usually had street names like Filthy, Loneheart, Rush, Honest Dave, Sidewalk, Leprechaun, and Loki, to name a few.

Oh, I could be scandalous myself back then. I even had a street name of my own, given to me by my good buddy Kyle Cantwell, aka "Filthy Nasty Von Rotten" (he's just a big goofball). He and I, together (but mostly

Kyle), came up with the hilarious street name (a toned-down version), Buddy Brown-Stains. We laughed hysterically through the process.

In coming to a place that was the lowest and darkest point in my life (which I never in a million years would have imagined), it took all that darkness for me to notice a light and something unique and special in each of these outcasts of society. In this, I am reminded of something my dear friend and Love Coach, Joe Paulicivic, gently and often says to me, *"Chuck, everything serves a purpose."*

"Yes indeed." I emphatically now agree. *"EVERYTHING serves a purpose!"*

As the stories within this book reveal, I've discovered that the sidewalks of my sometimes dark and hopeless world have offered me something I never expected nor saw coming. A revelation, discovering hearts of individuals who must daily make our concrete pedestrian pathways a resting spot, a temporary 'day camp,' even the closest thing to a living room, bedroom, or home. Is it possible these sidewalk dwellers are not what they may appear to be; that ne'er do well, good for nothing, or low life?

As I think about all the darkness I've lived through; struggles with my sexuality, drugs, addiction, self-worth, rejection, even perceived rejection (on my part) by family and peers, along with living with HIV since 1987, every bit of that darkness, has served to help me see the lack of understanding, compassion, and grace, not only in our society but in my own heart as well. The truth is that everyone, but mostly the misunderstood and ignorantly judged outcasts; we all need to know that we matter, are loved, and that someone truly cares about each of us.

One day I pondered the patches on Sidewalk's coveralls, her face tattoos, the fact she rarely gets to bathe, and that she is part of the *'Dirty Kid'* culture in the U.S. I was reminded of something I experienced in Uganda, Africa, while working in an orphanage, loving and caring for AIDS orphans in 2010. Many villagers and children simply wore rags and rarely got to bathe. There was a strong smell of body odor everywhere you went. All the things in the U.S. we consider to be 'bad' things and something we needed to "fix."

On our travels, we rode a small bus that shuttled us up and down dusty red dirt roads around the countryside and jungles of Kampala,

Uganda. We drove to villages where we fed the children and hopefully the adults when there was enough food. Also, riding back and forth from our hotel to Hope Children's Home in Gganda Village. It housed nearly 100 children orphaned due to the AIDS pandemic.

On one of those dusty red dirt road adventures, I have a very clear memory of peering out the window taking in all the sites and natural beauty of the African landscape and culture. There was a young African woman, tall and beautiful, walking alongside the road. She balanced a tall handwoven basket atop her head. With a blank expression, she stared only at the ground in front of her. She reminded me of me. The thought popped into my head, "Wave at her. Let her know you see her and appreciate her presence in the world."

I waved as we passed by, giving her my biggest smile ever. She glanced up at me with a blank expression. Quickly her eyes turned away, almost as if she were looking to see who I was waving at. I waved again. When she realized the waving of my hand was for her, a gorgeous smile spread like a beautiful golden sunrise across her face. Her eyes lit up as if to say, "Wow, someone noticed me, someone cares."

That precious smile, on what could be, at best, considered a 'sidewalk' along that dirt road, was to *light* my way to the rest of that sweet, love-filled journey throughout my stay in Uganda. Love was beginning to challenge my perspectives. I no longer noticed the odors nor saw the rags. I only saw their beautiful hearts and precious smiles. This newfound truth, slowly becoming clearer as I carried that light with me back home on a journey I never expected, graciously lit and guided by Love.

As my eyes began to open in 2016 to the beauty of the hearts in the street communities, I found myself writing about my adventures in posts on a social network. I simply wanted to share my joy with friends. The response was overwhelming. They wrote, "We feel like we are there with you, meeting your friends firsthand. I feel like I know them personally." And, "Can I come up to Portland and walk the streets with you someday? I'd like to meet these street folks. Maybe we could have a barbecue on the sidewalk and share food, music, and laughter." Others chimed in, feeling it was a great idea.

My heart, regarding the telling of these stories, is printed on a tiny slip of paper I found in a fortune cookie back in 2017. It was at a time when I was encouraged by all my friends on that social network to write this book.

That fortune simply read: *"Sharing little joys offers great hope to others."*

While writing the stories within this book, I found myself asking, "What is it that makes a sidewalk a sidewalk?" Is it just a formation of concrete laid alongside our city streets for pedestrians to travel to and fro, in the hustle and bustle of life; heading to work, appointments, or simply getting safely from point A to point B? Or are they just a constructed avenue, for the footfalls of despondent and weary consumers, and the lost-in-thought overworked business folk. Don't we all desire something more meaningful in life? Maybe, a break from the stress and droning monotony of our complicated socio-economic world? I've learned that most often, as I ponder these questions, the common ground is the absence of being present.

And during the writing process, I thought about my brief history on the streets and even in my forties, sowing wild oats, bar and club hopping, experimenting with drugs, and bouncing from relationship to relationship. Those memories kindled doubt and unworthiness within me as I worked to produce this project. It caused me to doubt the relationships I built with some of my friends on the streets. Thoughts crippled me with the pointed doubting question, "Were those relationships based on a hidden agenda or at times only drug-related friendships? Or were they based on truth and love?"

For much of my life, I believed the lie that I had no place in this world nor anything of value to offer. Yet, as my eyes have been opened to *see* the outcasts of our society in the *light* of Love, the outcasts have reminded me countless times that it *is my heart* that I have to offer and that it is deeply appreciated by every one of them.

Is it possible that each of these sidewalk dwellers is an opportunity for us sidewalk travelers to offer up a bit of ourselves and our time to truly live life as it was intended? An opportunity to be *present*, to *listen*, and to *help others* in need? And even more so, opportunity crying out to us, *"Store up your treasures in the Kingdom of Love rather than hoarding money and protecting worldly possessions."* This we often do, some of us even to the point of taking the life of another soul, one of Love's precious creations.

This journey has been a long and rough road, heartbreaking and dangerous. Yet, heartwarming and heart-winning. Joe's beautiful and loving wife, Denise Darlene Paulicivic, in her vast wisdom, shared this with me one day, *"We can only take people into the Kingdom of [Love] as far as we ourselves have gone."*

I thank Love for the journey and the length of that road. I cry out to hope that the world will one day walk this beautiful journey of *Love* together.

This old guy (how I often refer to myself throughout the book) came to learn through my personal experiences that the streets and sidewalks of our communities are paved virtually with the hearts of the outcasts of our society. The ones that are shunned, forgotten, broken, lost, and oppressed. Is it possible that the outcasts are precious gifts right before our very eyes if we'd only *open our eyes and see* with our *hearts; Hearts that see with the eyes of Love?* And aren't we ***all***, in some way, outcasts?

This journey has taken a hopelessly broken and lonely old guy, not only on a journey into the *hearts* of our street community, but into my own heart as well. No longer, *Buddy Brown-Stains*, I have discovered (through this journey orchestrated by Love), deeply hidden within my own heart, a compassionate, merciful, gracious, and unconditionally loving, *Poppa Chuck*.

Editors Preface

From the first page, I was hooked. My heart reached out to the people in the pages. I laughed with them, cried so many times, rejoiced with them, and held them in my heart. As I finished the book and thought back over the message, I was just floored! I couldn't even talk. I imagine every author's goal in writing such a book is to reach out into the world and touch the hearts of the readers, to leave a mark on the world. I know Poppa Chuck succeeded with me. This book made a difference. He helped me to see the beauty of the hearts of the people along his path.

I touched the edge of the homeless world myself once, and it was a frightening time for me. The loss of control, the feelings of helplessness and loneliness, breaks my heart even today. I think it would surprise many to know that there are more than a few who are just a paycheck away from that life and that it can come on so easily.

This is how I know the words are true. Because I lived a small corner of it, and it was the love of family, the kindness of strangers, and acceptance without question or judgment that helped me survive. I remember before my own experience how I feared the homeless. I never detested the people, but I know others did. I could see it and feel it. I realized they are just people, just like anyone else. Their circumstances are different, but they still fear, they still need love and acceptance, and their souls are still beautiful.

Thank you for writing this book, Poppa Chuck. I think the message is a gift to humanity. It offers a path to understanding and is so valuable.

Thank you for sharing that love is a language best shared with all. You have touched my life and made it better.

A grateful heart,

Marsha Fulton of MyPurplePen

Chapter One

"Homeless Encounters of the First Kind: Street Youth"

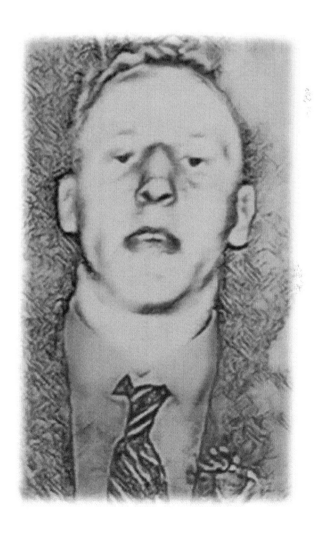

The aroma of barbecued hotdogs did little to distract me from the anxiety that worked to paralyze me as I stood on that street corner in downtown Portland back in 2003. Fight or flight was often my Plan B in these situations. I thought to myself, *"What the heck am I doing here?! I don't know what I'm doing!"* I remember working to suppress the anxiety. I tried simply being present, which is not an easy thing for me. I have lived my whole life with what is known as Androphobia, the "fear of men." Accepting this invitation to join a group of (even worse, religious) men, feeding a community of parade spectators at Portland's Annual Rose Festival Parade, was an opportunity to face that fear: albeit, a scary one.

To fit in and understand my job at the barbecue, I nervously listened while one of the men handed out hotdogs to whoever came by. It turned out that many were street youth and homeless. He handed out the churches' business cards with a smile along with the hotdogs stating he was from a local church.

Something didn't feel right. It felt like something was missing, at least for me. I began to wonder if these kids had ever felt loved? And, in all honesty, 'Are we loving these kids?' Then a profound question popped into my mind, 'Why am *I* doing this?' My answer was clear. I was doing it for them, for the hearts that needed food and drink, but more importantly, for each to know that someone cared. To not only show them through the sharing of food and drink, but to tell them that they truly mattered. Something I desired to hear my whole life.

It was like I was divinely prepared for the moment when a rough-looking and certainly streetwise kid with a skeptical look and a tone of judgment in his voice asked me point-blank (as I handed him a hotdog and coke), "Why are you doing this?" To this day, my response surprises me.

Looking up into his eyes, I smiled and said, "It's for you. We're doing this for you."

His reaction was a look of surprise. His demeanor changed in a split second, and he relaxed into relief from his own anxiety and the fear of judgment. "Thank you," he quietly said, looking into my eyes. His words were genuine and heartfelt. At that moment, I knew that he knew someone really cared about him, without an agenda or expectation.

Some of the kids asked me to pray for them. I was nervous and apprehensive. This was all new to me. Yet, I was deeply moved by how each one stood so still, closing their eyes tightly as if they'd waited a lifetime for this moment.

I really didn't know what I was doing. I just did it. First asking permission, then placing one hand on their shoulder and the other gently atop their head. I have no idea why I did that. But I do remember their tears, their smiles, and hugs. I was overwhelmed by how grateful each was for serving them, for loving them, for offering hope, but most of all, for a much-needed father's hug.

Three years went by before I was to have another, yet closer, encounter with a street person. I was five years into loving my job at Fanno Creek Clinic in SW Portland. Not only my job but my coworkers as well, like "Nicholessa" Thurman, she is more like a daughter to me. Even her husband Bill and I became good friends and workout partners at the gym. We supported one another in the many ways men do by confiding in one another, encouraging, and pointing out each other's strengths.

Life was good, even wonderful, and magical until I neared my 50th birthday. I don't know why the anxiety and clinical depression kicked in so harshly, but they did. My mental health rapidly declined in just two short weeks. It was not long before I was unable to work full time.

Enter the son of two of my favorite patients (Ron and Patt Bottaro) at Fanno Creek Clinic. Patt and I bonded over a phone conversation one afternoon. I worked the phones at the time, and fortunately, her call came to me. Patt was in distress, sharing that her son was living with HIV, experiencing several complications. She'd heard that Dr. Gregg Coodley was a prominent HIV Specialist in Portland's medical community. More than anything, Patt needed comfort and reassurance. I was grateful to receive her call because I knew I could help. I shared with Patt right away that I completely related to her son's situation, for I, too, lived with HIV. Our phone conversation must have lasted 20 minutes or more. Even though Dr. Coodley was not accepting new patients at the time, he agreed to see Ron and Patt's son, Scott.

I made an effort to meet Scott when he arrived for his first appointment. Scott is a fun-loving guy, just four years younger than me. He dealt with a lot at that point in his life. We got acquainted through our brief interactions at the clinic. He knew I loved his parents dearly. We became fast friends. Scott was often homeless or couch surfing. Ron and Patt lived way out in West Linn. Scott liked being downtown near his friends. There were times I would drive him out to his parent's home to visit. I hung out with them many times. It was not long afterward that Patt 'adopted' me. She would call me often to check on me. That precious woman truly loved me like a son. I honestly believe that Ron did too.

Scott stayed with me on occasion, always keeping me in stitches, especially one night while I was falling asleep. He had several characters he made up; two of them were children. As a kid, he did this to make his mom smile and laugh during the difficult times in life. I learned that two of the characters were eight-year-old Savay and six-year-old Billy.

The first night I heard Scott go into character, I was almost asleep when I heard a little boy's voice whisper, "*Stop it!*"

Then another child's voice, in disagreement, whispered, "*No, you stop it!*" Scott had me in tears laughing so hard as these two characters continued their banter, battling for their mom to side with one of them. Scott not only has a great sense of humor but a heart of gold.

Months went by, Scott eventually was approved for Section Eight housing. We maintained our friendship and often checked in with one another. He knew depression all too well. There were many occasions when Scott demanded I come to stay at his place. He did not want me to be alone, especially at Christmas time. Scott was a *Love-send*.

I remember the day Scott had me tag along with him to a friend's apartment on West Burnside Street downtown. It was there Scott introduced me to the first street kid I started to hang out with and quickly grew to love.

The Heart of Chris Gibbons

Chris is quite the character, having lived on the streets since the age of 14. When we met, Chris was 32 and, yes, on the streets, someone up into their 50s or even 60s might be considered a "kid." Twenty-two years is a long time to be homeless. Chris was very private about his life, to begin with, but as I offered him a reprieve from the streets, giving him the futon to sleep on (on many occasions), I began to learn a bit about the hearts of people I did not yet understand.

Chris is wild at heart in an endearing way. Fluorescent blue, twelve-inch spiked mohawks, racing around downtown Portland doing tricks on his bike, and getting into all kinds of mischief, were common characteristics of his teen years on the streets. It was his way of having fun and coping with a life he never saw coming and was certainly not allowing it to take him down.

He shared with me that at the age of 16, he entered a Bike Mechanic Training Course with Community Cycling in Portland, one of many accomplishments he is proud of. Not long afterward, Chris was given a plant nursery in SE Portland off Wichita and Johnson Creek roads, with a greenhouse to boot. For a couple of years, he enjoyed life owning and operating that nursery.

His dad lay dying in the hospital when Chris was 18. He loved his father but failed to visit him in time. This is a regret Chris carries with him to this day. Six months afterward, on December 20, 1994, Chris' mom died. Devastated, his whole life had fallen apart.

There are many reasons that Chris has been on the streets. Being raised by parents struggling with addiction, I suppose, even dealing drugs to cope with the disease of addiction was a huge factor. Chris struggles with abandonment issues, depression, and hopelessness. He also carries sadness, guilt, and shame with him. For he, at times, abandoned others in his life as well.

Chris and I often watched movies together at my place. It was through watching one of my favorite films, "Life as a House," with the message of redemption in a lost and damaged father/son relationship, that I learned about Chris' empathic and sensitive heart. I sob uncontrollably every time I see this film, connecting with my heart, allowing myself to feel the sorrow as I relate to a young man who hates his father, then the joy of a son falling in love again with the father he'd lost long ago as a child when his parents divorced. I witnessed Chris' heartstrings pulled to the point where he shed what seemed like a bucket load of tears the night we first watched that film together. I learned Chris connects with his heart in the same way that I do.

For Chris, opportunities to be inside like this are a rare but welcome relief and distraction from the harsh realities of living life on the streets.

Not an easy life. It can be filled with danger and loneliness, as well as unexpected beauty, like my good buddy, Chris.

Early on in our friendship, I quickly learned Chris wears his heart on his sleeve. Even when that "sleeve" is filthy dirty, his heart is right there in all the mess, with Chris doing the best he can. Especially with the cards he's been dealt in life. He works to enjoy life and make the best of it, but depression often works to derail him. Something I am all too well familiar with.

As Chris gradually shared bits and pieces of his life, I wondered how he had made it through all the trauma. Hearing his story, one that is completely different from that of my own traumatic story, I was learning that giving someone the benefit of the doubt is a positive tool in better understanding and being a friend to others. At the time, I wasn't aware of the depth of this new understanding. It was beginning to change my whole perspective on life and reveal the power of loving others unconditionally.

As 2006 came to a close, Chris was spending more time at my apartment, settling in on the futon, for winter was on its way. I really didn't want to be alone. I hated that feeling. I wondered if Chris hated it too.

During some of our talks, Chris admitted through tears and hopelessness that he would never get married or have kids. He felt unattractive, his teeth nearly all gone from a pool room brawl when he was 21 (attacked by a couple of guys armed with pool cues). He had resigned himself from ever having a driver's license, with several major outstanding citations that needed to be cleared up. And as a former felon, it was difficult for Chris to get a job. Even the possibility of ever having his own place to live seemed impossible to him. Despair loomed over my buddy like a dark cloud far too often. I did not feel sorry for Chris; I knew he didn't want that. But something inside me knew that Chris was wrong.

One day when Chris fell into despair and depression again, I offered him these thoughts to help him consider the possibilities. "Chris," I confidently said to him. "I guarantee you, one day, you will have every one of these things that you feel you lack. Mark my words."

Chris and I were on some kind of parallel back then. I often fell into despair as well as doubting my self-worth. Anxiety had become a new enemy in my life the year before. I didn't even know at the time what was wrong with me. In December, I left my position at the medical office and spiraled hopelessly into a deep depression, then self-medicated out of control. I don't even remember if I quit my job or I was fired. I just stopped going to work.

Without an income, food was scarce at my place. A church helped pay a few months of my rent. One day Chris told me that he was going out to get food. He did not ask nor expect me to go along with him. He simply headed out late one morning, arriving back at my place five hours later. I slept nearly the whole time he was gone.

There was a loud knock at the door. I got up from my bed, walked out into the living room, and opened the front door. It was Chris carrying two large boxes, one stacked atop the other. "Here is some of the food," he said, putting the boxes on the floor in the kitchen. "Come on; there are five more boxes up the street at the bus stop. We should get them right away before someone else does."

I wondered what the heck was going on? I slipped on my shoes without question, following my buddy up the hill to Capitol Hwy. It was cold out. Chris wore only a lightweight jacket. "Where did he get all this food?" I wondered to myself. "And how did he get it all here?"

At the bus stop (it was dark now), Chris gave a sigh of relief, "Whew … they're all still here. I was nervous there for a minute."

I picked up a medium size box filled with all kinds of canned, boxed, and fresh foods, as well as pastries, candy bars, and milk. Chris stacked one box on top of another to carry back to the apartment; they were large boxes compared to the one I carried. We then headed down into the cul-de-sac and through the gate to my apartment. Setting his boxes down, Chris said. "I'll go back and get the other two. See you in a minute," he promised, flashing me a smile.

And not much more than a minute later, Chris was now back inside my place, setting that last box on the kitchen table and locking the door to my apartment. "That was one helluva trip!" he exclaimed, wiping his forehead.

"Where the heck did you get all of this food, Chris?!" I asked.

"Oh, it's a foodbank way out in SE Portland. They always give out a ton of food, and you need it." Chris was pleased and proud of himself.

"Chris!" I exclaimed almost with disbelief. "But how did you get it here?"

"Well, that was the interesting part," Chris began. Then his story unfolded. "I took a couple of boxes at a time from the food bank to the nearest bus stop. Then went back to get the others. Each time I got on or off a bus, I'd take a couple at a time then go back to get the others until I had them all together. Then I waited for the next bus, which took me to the next bus, and the next, doing the same thing each time. A couple of the drivers were annoyed. They scowled or glared at me. Others looked at me like I was crazy. But I didn't care." He shrugged, "I just wanted to get this food to you."

Tears welled up in my eyes as I realized Chris has a very giving heart that enjoys helping others. His work ethic is strong, but his work opportunities were rare. I gave Chris a big hug thanking him. We both rested well that night. Chris was satisfied with his accomplishments for the day (helping his friend and bringing food to the table). I was proud of Chris and grateful to witness some of his amazing character traits.

One of my favorite oddities about Chris is when he bathes or showers. While washing his feet (and the dude's got huge feet for someone just 5'9" tall), he always laughs out loud. It's like a joyful and delightful laugh like a child getting tickled. On one occasion, a friend stopped by to visit. I explained Chris was in the shower and feigned concern stating, "If he doesn't laugh while he's in the shower, I'm going to be pissed!"

"What?" They asked with a puzzled look.

With a smile, I said, "If Chris doesn't laugh while he's showering, it means he didn't wash his feet." Sure enough, just a few moments later, we hear Chris delightfully laughing in the shower. I called out to him through the bathroom door, "Thank you for washing your feet, Chris!" And, again, we hear him laugh.

Chris is funny as heck and a natural-born storyteller. He passionately tells stories of his wild adventures in life, spinning those tales taller than Metroplex, the tallest of all the Transformer characters. Here I will share one of our hilariously funny adventures *together*.

"The Horrifying and Hilarious: Helvetia Tavern Turd Tale"

It was summer; God only knows what year it was. It doesn't matter; this tale is timeless, standing on its own. I invited Chris to join me on a day trip to the Oregon Coast, a rare opportunity for both of us.

Driving from Portland to Cannon Beach, I suggested we stop at the Helvetia Tavern (best known throughout the country as one of the ***Top Ten best burgers in the nation***). I'd been there only once before with my family in December one year. We had just visited a tree farm to get a Christmas tree for the holiday. The burgers at Helvetia Tavern are ginormous and delicious! It would be Chris' first time there; I knew he would love it. Well, until nature came calling.

Once we were parked, we went inside, placing our orders. We ordered burgers, fries, and Chris got a beer. I ordered my favorite root beer, Henry Weinhard's, since I was driving. We went through the backdoor to the outdoor dining area behind the tavern, seating ourselves at a picnic table anxiously awaiting our meal.

What a beautiful day! Everything was perfect for our day trip, the weather, road tunes, feeling free, enjoying being out of downtown, out in the countryside. Soon our order arrived, and we voraciously attacked those beautiful burgers. Suddenly, Chris exclaimed, "Where's the restroom? I gotta go, *NOW!*"

'Yikes!' I thought to myself. I hope he makes it in time.

"Chris, run inside and ask someone. It's probably just inside the door." He got up, and off he went. I sat there for what seemed like way too long for any person to relieve themself. I wondered if he was okay or if someone should check on him. I certainly didn't want to! We had lived together on and off for a couple of years. I always let him stay with me when he needed to be inside, which was often, and I never minded having his company.

But as a result, he and I were all too familiar with each other's toileting traumas.

I finished my burger, wondering if Chris was going to finish his when he returned, but at that very moment, his head shot out the backdoor of the tavern. He whispered loudly to me, "*Chuck! Come on! We gotta go ....* ***NOW!!!***"

"*Oh crap!*" I unknowingly, yet fittingly, said out loud as I got up, grabbing our trash and the remainder of Chris' burger.

"*No, leave it, Chuck!*" He whispered, desperately and even louder. "*Come on! HURRY! PLEEEASE!*"

'Oh, God!' I thought to myself, 'What has he done now?!' The worst thing I could think was that he took a couple of hits of weed in the restroom, and maybe the smell was overpowering that of the aroma of a deep fryer, burgers, and fries. Little did I know there was an aroma alright, but it was (as Chris tells it) flowing out of a toilet onto the restroom floor and out into the hallway, heading into the dining room of the Tavern. At least, that was Chris's fear.

I left his burger on the table. Chris still had his head poking out of the doorway, but seemed to be desperately looking for another way out, certainly not wanting to head back inside where he and the flood of excrement would both be discovered and identified as co-sponsors of his ensuing nightmare.

Thankfully, I had already paid for our lunch. Once we were buckled in, Chris wove that tale like a seasoned pro, scaring even the crap out of me while we drove onto the highway, escaping into the forests of Oregon's Coast Range. I am certain Chris may have embellished a bit regarding the extent of an overflowing toilet. But his story overflowed with morbid comic relief. I could barely drive as Chris made my side ache with laughter!

The Wild and Worrisome Wildland Firefighter

In the spring of 2007, Chris excitedly informed me that he was applying and testing to serve as a Wildland Firefighter for an outfit based in Pendleton, Oregon. Part of me was surprised, but part of me was not. I was more proud of him than anything. This was something Chris would do. When it comes to adventure, he has *NO FEAR!*

He took a brief training course and easily passed the required Pack Test, which included an arduous three-mile hike with a 45-pound pack in 45 minutes. Piece of cake for my young and scrappy street buddy. It was not long before Chris was off to Pendleton, where he awaited dispatch orders with a crew of guys and gals to battle his first forest fire.

Chris called a couple of times a week with updates on his adventures. I remember a day he called telling me how much people appreciated all that the firefighters were doing. This happened *EVERYWHERE* they went.

"Chuck, we are starving after fighting fires all day. When we stop at restaurants, we pack our whole crew around several tables, sometimes filling the whole restaurant. When we start to order, the manager and owners will have none of that and won't let us pay our bills. They give us steaks, potatoes, seafood, and all kinds of great food I hardly ever get to eat. And the desserts are awesome! I've never experienced anything like this before! People appreciate me instead of treating me like I am always worthless and a burden to them," he started to choke up. "It's like I'm doing something good and worthwhile for the first time in my life. I almost don't know how to act."

"Dude, Chris! This is what I've been trying to tell you. You're an awesome person with a big heart, and people see that. They are seeing the real you." I was grateful to encourage Chris at that moment, nurturing his self-worth, and a healthy sense of pride.

A couple of months later, I received a phone call from Chris that was not like the others; in fact, it nearly tore my heart out. "Chuck," came Chris' faint voice. "There was an accident. I'm in the hospital."

The words hit me like a ton of bricks. Words that I hoped would be avoided during Chris' firefighting gigs. "Chris, are you okay?" I asked, fearing the answer.

"I'm okay," he responded, still in a whisper. "I got caught in a fire. It's difficult for me to talk right now. The lining in my lungs is burned. I'll call you in a couple of days when I can talk. Ask people to pray for me, please."

"Sure, Chris," I promised. "I'll call people at The Well (a fellowship he and I were familiar with) right away. They'll want to know. You rest and call me as soon as you're able to speak without it being painful. You don't want to make it worse."

"I will. I gotta go, gotta get some rest. I'll talk to you later." He hung up the phone. I sat staring off into space. I wondered what the heck happened that Chris got caught in a fire? Time would tell. I knew when Chris could talk, he'd want to tell me the story right away. Chris rocks adventure. There's no doubt about that.

Three days later, he called again. "I can talk a little better now, but I'm still in the hospital. Well, it's more like an old folk's home. There are five hospital rooms. Everyone is *old* here, Chuck. They use this place as a hospital as well. There's only one doctor, and he's only in this area three days a week. *It's like the Twilight Zone here, Chuck!*" Chris made himself sound like he was desperate for an escape.

I felt better now that Chris made me laugh. But his situation told me, wherever he was, he was out in Podunk *nowhere*. I hoped he was getting good care. Working for Oregon Health Sciences University at the time, I was somewhat of a hospital snob. I imagined Chris fit to be tied, desperately working toward either an escape or a quick recovery. I hoped for the latter.

"You want me to tell you what happened?" he asked, then baited me with these words: "It was crazy; I thought I was a goner!"

I thought to myself, 'Either Chris was in the mood to entertain me, or it would be a very real and scary retelling of the events that led up to his being in the hospital.' I gave Chris a very apprehensive, "Okay ... go ahead. I'm all ears."

Chris began his tale, and I was indeed not disappointed. "Well, we were fighting a fire. I was instructed to help secure the safety of a cabin on the hillside. There were trees way up the hill that were in flames and to the east and west. When I got to the cabin, everything was clear until I walked around the backside. At first, everything was clear there too. There was no indication of a fire anywhere. But then, **BOOM!** I heard these explosions all around me and looked up to see every tree surrounding me exploding into flames! I didn't know what the hell I was going to do. I called out for help, but no one answered."

Chris continued, "The flames were closing in on me. There was fire and smoke **EVERYWHERE!** I could barely see; I was coughing, and it

12

was getting difficult to breathe. I thought maybe I should run as fast as I could through the flames to the cabin but knew I would burn to death if I did. I didn't know what to do. Then all of a sudden, I heard this LOUD voice from the sky yell, *'GET DOWN ...NOW!!!!'* That's when I heard a helicopter overhead."

"I immediately crouched down close to the ground, and all of a sudden, it was like a million billion raindrops all gathered themselves together like one big flood from the sky, dousing me and all the trees around me. The voice boomed from the sky above me again, *'TAKE A DEEP BREATH AND RUN ...NOW!!!'* And so, I did."

"I didn't have enough air in my lungs to last till I came out of the flames on the other side where my crew was waiting to rescue me. I took a deep breath while still running through the flames and smoke. It singed the hair in the lining of my lungs so they couldn't get the mucus and stuff up and out of me. I was still alive, not burned, but unable to breathe. I didn't tell my captain right away. But he kept a close eye on me for the next day or so, then took me to the hospital."

Chris stopped there. He was silent, his tale having spent him. I was overcome. I began sobbing. I didn't want him to hear me. It was a deep, mournful sob that came from the depth of my heart, my *father-heart*. I realized my good buddy, who'd helped me so much in the last year, well ...I'd almost lost him. I continued to sob quietly, even pulling the phone away from my mouth so he couldn't hear me, then told Chris I needed to go. I didn't know what to do with my emotions. After I hung up, it took me a while to collect myself. When I did, I was grateful that Love brought my buddy through the smoke and flames, through all that danger, keeping him safe.

"*Coming safely out of danger*" defines Chris's whole life. Walking through danger as a street youth time after time and coming out on the other side, maybe unable to catch his breath for a moment, but he is always brought safely through it.

During that summer of firefighting, Chris began dating an old girlfriend from his teen years. By 2010 they were married. Gina had two daughters from a previous marriage. Chris now had his driver's license, owned a huge F10 4-door pickup, had a dog named Curly (he adores Chris), and a cat named Mystery. Chris drove the girls to school in the mornings while Gina was off to work. Then picked them up at school in the afternoon. Chris now had a home and family, everything I promised he would have one day. And the best part, Chris now has a full set of teeth and a beautiful smile.

The spring of 2011 was a chaotic and traumatic time in my family's life. My mom and younger brother had heart attacks three weeks apart. Two weeks later, my dad fell at home, completely snapping off the femur in his right hip—this required surgery. Dad was unable to participate in his physical therapy. As a result, and with the complications of his blindness and 30 years living with emphysema, he was bedridden and rapidly declining in a nursing home. Then my sister broke her foot. I worked on a farm with developmentally disabled adults during this time. After work, I'd visit Dad at the nursing home, then check in on Mom recuperating at their house, then finally head home. My self-care sucked at the time. I was taking care of everyone but me. I was exhausted and depleted.

Living in my hometown that year, I had to drive to Portland to see my specialty healthcare providers. On one of those trips, it was May of 2012, and I decided to drop in on Chris, Gina, and the girls. Bella and D'ahna were like granddaughters to me. I always look forward to their smiles and a bit of lighthearted conversation with Chris and Gina.

As our visit winded down, Chris and I walked downstairs to the parking lot. I got in my car, rolled down the window of my Ford Focus to finish our chat, then confided in Chris now that we were alone. "Chris, I'm barely hanging on, man. Things are so bad that I want to get high."

Chris shot back without hesitating, *"No, Chuck, you're not going there. That's not the answer!"* Chris opened his garage door, and I got out of my car. He was willing to listen, so we sat down inside the garage, continuing to have a long chat. It's what guys do. Chris spent two hours talking me out of a relapse.

Chris spent nearly three years in prison from 2018-20. An explosion rocked the Beaverton apartment he lived in with his wife and two daughters. It happened during Chris' failed attempt at making hash oil in the kitchen while his wife and kids were in their rooms. His face and hands were severely burned. He admits it was really stupid. He just wanted something to help ease the pain of a degenerative condition affecting his back, shoulders, and neck. His sister lives with the same painful condition.

When Chris was released from prison into a halfway house, he came to visit right away. He enjoyed sharing stories of his prison experience with me and what he learned about life through that experience. The following is a note written to him by his "cellie," Nate, just before Chris was released from prison. It offers a peek into the beauty that others see in Chris and how easily he captures their hearts, just by being his wild and charming self.

"Chris, It's time for the next chapter in our life's story. Don't forget the one we just completed because it's an essential part of what comes next. Try to find something of value in each day and run with it. I'm glad our stories shared a chapter. Thanks for contributing to my successes. I hope I did the same for you. I pray that your family is made whole in time. Trust in the process and let it flow at its own pace while you work hard at becoming the best 'Chris' you can be. You're worth investing in, so never stop sowing the seeds of your personal growth journey."

~Nate

Chris's story has taken a lot of twists and turns since his release from prison in 2019. His wife left him while he was incarcerated. Chris spent a few months in the halfway house then was back on the streets for 18 months living in a homeless camp. As of this publication, Chris is now housed in the Goose Hollow neighborhood of downtown Portland. He has a spacious one-bedroom apartment overlooking the Providence Park soccer stadium. Needless to say, I am very proud of him.

Chris has been excited about this project from the beginning, encouraging me all along the way. There are countless other amazing stories about Chris's life I could include, so when I finished this segment, I messaged Chris. "Dude, your life is such that I think the readers might want to learn a lot more about you. You're a good writer. You should consider writing a book about your life." Chris likes that idea. I will encourage *him* all the way!

"HEY! My blue-eyed Burrito Buddy! Our adventures are sick! And you be the SCHITT!!!! I love you, man. ALWAYS WILL!!! Bless you, and thank you for your enduring friendship!"

~Chuckles (as you so endearingly call me)

Little did I know that the brief encounter with street youth and un-expected relationships with Chris and Scott would be the precursors to yet another encounter with an endearing, cunning yet charismatic, and larger-than-life character that would further challenge what I thought I knew about the homeless. I was soon to learn what lengths those on the streets will go to care for those they love.

Chapter Two

"Homeless Encounters of the Second Kind: A Ray of Light in the Dark"

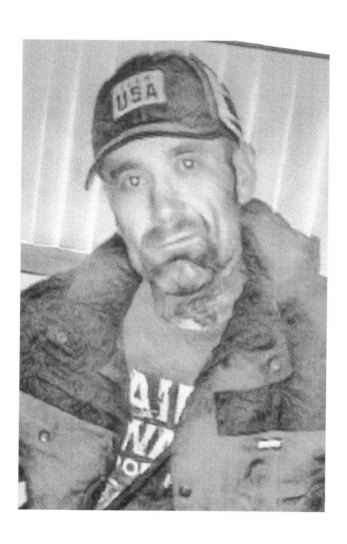

In February 2015, I met Ray on a sidewalk in the Hollywood District of NE Portland, not far from where I lived. He was preparing to board his black Norco single-speed bicycle with a trailer attached. Ray is a handsome, scrappy, and well-built guy in his mid-thirties. He wore a black shirt with "Police" printed on it in bold white letters, black jeans, and a black baseball cap with "Police" printed on it as well. He also wore an impressive black vest with pockets all over it and a plethora of bicycle tools in the pockets. I was certain Inspector Gadget would be proud.

After smile-woven introductions, Ray shared with me that he'd been homeless for five years and currently camped under the east side of the Burnside Bridge. He briefly explained what his daily life was like; living under a bridge and completing his arduous tasks and routines while camped on the sidewalk. He spent a great deal of time helping his neighbors when they were in need. Ray explained he had an uncanny ability to come across particular items whenever someone needed something. Ray called it "treasure hunting." The items were always free, and his fellow campers were ever so grateful for Ray's help.

Nothing about our conversation, his words, or demeanor hinted at displeasure with being homeless. He appeared to be fairly happy to me and making the best of his situation.

By the end of our talk, which lasted about 45 minutes, we agreed to meet again for coffee. I'd mentioned to Ray that I was a Peer Support Specialist working with homeless men. I hoped that maybe I could help him, or at least encourage and support him in some way.

Ray and I did meet again. Our conversations often centered around the loss of our families, jobs, and failures in life. I suppose Ray was the first person I was honest with about my depression, anxiety, cognitive, and memory challenges. It wasn't easy admitting that to another person.

I was five months into my new half-time position as a Peer Support Specialist working for a local non-profit. And like all the jobs I had in the past, I loved my job and the people I worked with. I saw this job as the perfect position for me. In this position, all of the struggles and challenges in my life were now useful tools. No longer were the mental health issues and my history with addiction hindrances in my life. It was all working to help others like me by walking alongside them in approaching housing, medical, and recovery opportunities.

Before I knew it, I was asked to take a position with Multnomah County as a Navigator. A huge step up in my field. I'd still be working for the non-profit half-time, but now I'd be working full-time with the added 20 hours a week at the County Health Center. I was honored and elated. My life was perfect. I need only go through the interview process as a technicality.

Yet, as amazing as my life was at the time, something was wrong. I became very forgetful and struggled with anxiety attacks while working with a couple of peers (aka clients). There were two in particular that had aggressive entitlement issues. I soon found they were also verbally and emotionally abusive, which awakened emotional distress within me. Something I hadn't experienced since I was a teen.

One of my peers had a seizure during a phone conversation. I discovered he'd been in the seizure for a couple of minutes, but the House Manager at the Adult Care Facility was not paying attention, misinterpreting the seizure as a behavior. He almost died.

Then an important relationship with a family member crumbled before my very eyes. Anxiety attacks reared their ugly head, and depression kicked in harshly. Everything seemed to be falling apart. My heart was breaking. Then the straw that broke the camel's back hit me hard. I learned that my dear friend, Scott Bottaro, died of a brain tumor the month before. I was not there for my friend and didn't get to say goodbye. A deep depression took hold. I stopped going to work. That job I had loved so much now seemed an impossible task. My employment capabilities were severely compromised. The emotions over the loss of my ability to hold down even a part-time job were destroying me. I was devastated.

I began seeing a psychiatrist. We learned that I was experiencing PTSD, cognitive challenges, and increased anxiety. I was no longer diagnosed with Clinical Depression; it was now Severe Depressive Disorder. They did an MRI of the brain and put me on a lot of new meds. The MRI results came back fine; however, I was not.

But then there was Ray. We'd grown to be good friends. Ray showed a great amount of compassion for me. He often stayed at my place, sleeping on the couch, so I wasn't alone. He was the only person I felt I could trust back then. He attended doctor appointments with me whenever I felt I couldn't go it alone. The support Ray provided led to him being my go-to person.

Anxiety, Compassion, and Pillows

Anxiety attacks were like monsters that entered the room of my life. As if I didn't have enough monsters in my life already. I wasn't feeling safe *anywhere*. Not that it made things any better, but beginning to understand what I was dealing with, helped me to begin to have compassion for myself.

Soon Ray was spending every night on my couch. My psychiatrist, seeing how Ray helped to calm me, wrote a Doctor's Order recommending Ray be allowed to stay with me full time for a couple of months. Ray was essentially my caregiver. He understood the anxiety attacks and soon helped to keep me grounded. If Ray had somewhere to be, he let me know how long he would be gone, which helped to keep me stable. He always spoke to me calmly and gently, which is really what I needed with the depression and anxiety.

One evening, I was in bed early due to a really bad anxiety attack, hoping it would subside. Ray came into my room to check on me, letting me know he needed to go out for a while. I told him I couldn't calm down, that it was freaking me out. Ray calmly said, "I'm not sure what to do to help you."

I lied to him, saying it was okay, that I'd be fine. Ray left the room but came back a couple of minutes later. Without saying a word, he had grabbed his heavy king-size down comforter off of the couch and brought it into my room. Ray threw it over the top of me. I had six pillows on my bed. First, he shoved the comforter down under me from my shoulders to my feet, all around me like a cocoon. Then he grabbed all the pillows and shoved them tight all around me as well. *INSTANTLY,* the anxiety melted away. It was remarkable!

My eyes teared up, maybe because I realized someone cared, having the determination to help in any way possible even though not knowing how. I was overwhelmed, mostly because I knew that I truly had a great friend. With relief and surprise, I asked Ray, "How did you know to do that?"

"I don't know. It just came to me. So, you're okay?"

"Yeah, man. I'm better than okay. Thank you for being here for me and being so patient." With that, Ray smiled, he shut my bedroom door, and I fell fast asleep.

Ray is highly intelligent, witty, and funnier than heck. He is like a *creative beast* and loves entertaining others non-stop. During his stay with me, he built bicycles (one for me), made knives, and even a machete to help with clearing brush for camps. He is also a sketch artist, tattoo artist, harmonica player, woodworker, caretaker, martial arts instructor, and good friend. He made me go on bike rides with him, which helped boost my endorphins and was amazing therapy for me.

After a couple of months, Ray's stay at my place came to an end. He was back on the streets looking for a camp. He went back to his previous camp under the Burnside Bridge but was displaced shortly thereafter due to a Sweep by the Portland Police. Ray was left with no choice but to try to make the best of it, find another spot, and make it his home. He ended up in his tent on a muddy slope near the freeway in North Portland. He was now exposed to all the elements in a rat-infested camp, a place no one would ever want to call home.

Ray would often call me at night. Most nights, he did not want to be alone. This amazing tough, strong, and independent man wanted his friend around. It was a rarity that I'd ever tell him I couldn't. As soon as I hung up the phone, I'd get dressed, heading out to the camp to keep Ray company. We would laugh a lot, sometimes cry together, and I got to hear more of Ray's fascinating adventures in life.

There was a small group of men camped on the hillside under the trees above Ray's camp. The trees offered shelter from Oregon's rainstorms and the heat of our summer. A man named Raven spearheaded the growth of this camp. Raven is a born leader. He and his husband, Dash, were soon concerned for Ray's safety and health. So, they invited him to live up on the hillside where it was somewhat dry and where there was a bird's eye view to help keep them all safe from intruders.

It wasn't long before this muddy slope began to house other homeless individuals. Ray soon got to know them all, and so did I. In addition to Raven and Dash, there was Leprechaun, Marty, and Donut, along with many others. That homeless camp on Greeley Avenue and the hearts within it became my safe place.

The Growth of the Hazelnut Grove Camp

As the months went by, miracles helped to shape the camp on that rat-infested slope. Out of the mud, there grew a caring community of tent dwellers. The camp was named Hazelnut Grove. Just months after Ray moved there, news reporters came to interview the camp residents weekly and sometimes daily. They interviewed Raven (now the camp liaison with city officials) and often interviewed Ray and others. Mayoral candidates spent a couple of nights each at the camp to better understand the need first hand. The city then rallied around the Hazelnut Grove Camp to prove that solutions are possible and that the homeless are not abandoned.

Ray designed and built the first tiny home at Hazelnut Grove in the summer of 2016. I got to be Ray's first helper. Ray scavenged for discarded pallets on his bicycle. He spent hours dismantling each one, salvaging the wood, and as many nails as possible. Nails became like gold to Ray. I learned quickly that I'd better not lose one of his precious nails, or I'd get 'the look.' Just a look that was clever and funny, a 'what did I tell you' look. Ray never scolded me. His patience was always intact.

There were horror stories for sure at the camp. Mostly it involved the rats on the hillside. Ray built flooring out of dismantled pallets to put his tent on in preparation for winter. He used a level to get the floor just right so rainwater would flow under the flooring and down the hill. But it also provided a space for rats to weather out of the storms. They roamed around the camp seeking out food, shelter, and stealing Ray's tools, along with anything that fell through the cracks of the flooring. I chuckle to myself now, but it's almost like Ray created a space just for the rats to have a much more exciting and fulfilling life. More often than not, the rats got into fights right underneath my sleeping bag. It felt and sounded like they were right next to me. I wasn't able to sleep much those nights. Neither was Ray, but that was the norm for him.

In the evenings on hot days, Ray headed out on his bike with the trailer attached, going to the local fast-food businesses. They all donated bucket loads of ice every day. He always shared the ice with his fellow campers. Ray often needed to find a place to charge his cell phone. Along the way, he scouted for discarded building supplies while I stayed at his camp to keep an eye on his tools and power equipment used for construction.

To build his tiny homes, Ray scavenged for building supplies, using pallets, wood products, and 'free box' items that Portland homeowners put out at the curbside. There are often household items, clothing, and more for whoever might have a need. Ray carried loads of all kinds of things on his bicycle AND on foot, oftentimes working into the wee hours of the night, even though he was exhausted physically and emotionally. He never gave up. Many nights, when Ray felt he couldn't deal with the pain of being alone any longer, he shared with me the sadness and pain he lives with; he misses his daughter, Savannah, and son, Nathaniel. But his reason for not sleeping was because of his dreams. He would dream about his kids and wake up missing them terribly. "I don't want to sleep and dream about them," he admitted through tears. "I feel like I let them down. I feel like I've failed as a father." It filled him with more regret and remorse. He would rather work endless hours than be lost in thought over the loss of his family.

I assured Ray that if his kids were to know him as I do, they would be the proudest kids in the world. If they could see their dad through this old guy's eyes, they would marvel at how amazing, creative, talented, passionate, driven, and resourceful this man is. There is no doubt in my mind.

Eventually, a nearby home re-store supplied Ray with everything he needed to build several prototype tiny homes. He worked night and day for almost two years. Ray's desire for perfection drove him to continually improve on and redesign the prototypes. Some days would be 'demolition day' on Ray's agenda. That's when he tore down a structure or parts of it in order to reconstruct a prototype. You might say Ray is a little OCD… or maybe, a *LOT*, admittedly and endearingly so.

In less than three years, I witnessed that camp grow from a tattered tarp and tent slum to an almost magical tiny home (gated) community with electricity and plumbing for a small sink in each cottage. Some cottages had hand-made quilts on the beds. There were gardens, a library, mess hall, clothing and blanket resource tents, and so much more.

Briars, Nettles, Machetes, and Ray to the Rescue!

On sunny days we sometimes left our bikes and went on adventures in my car. One of those adventures was to a beach on the Columbia River. We hung out for quite some time, relaxing on the beach. I decided I needed some shade, so I went for a walk on my own, up in a wooded area, thinking it was late afternoon and that I had plenty of time before dusk, not realizing it was actually early evening.

I enjoyed the relief from the hot sun in the shade of the trees as I walked along paths lined with ferns, blackberries, and brush. There were all kinds of plants I was not familiar with. It was nice being out in nature and away from the city. Because of the heat, I wore just my jeans, no shirt, and no shoes.

After about 30 minutes, I realized I should head back down to the beach, but it seemed the light was changing. Then I noticed the mosquitoes. "Crap!" I thought. 'I better get the heck outta here.' Especially since I deal with night blindness and didn't have my glasses (for serious nearsightedness), I'd left them on the beach with Ray.

But it was too late. Dusk was coming quickly; I had a hard time making out the trail. I was veering off into the blackberry thickets. Blackberry thorns pierced the bottoms of my feet with each step. It was extremely painful. I tried to walk up out of the woods, but it seemed I was getting myself deeper into trouble.

Then the mosquitoes really started biting me; I realized I better call out for help. I wondered if things could get any worse, and then came the nettles, flying through the air, stinging my chest, head, and back any time I moved a few steps. Besides being in a great deal of pain, I was getting a little scared. I started to holler for help.

24

It took about 20 minutes of yelling "HELP" at the top of my lungs before someone heard me. Eventually, a man came down the hillside to help me out. But, now, it was completely dark out. He was stuck along with me and couldn't see a way out either.

This is where the story gets comical. I suddenly realized my cell phone was in my back pocket (I always kept it in the front). I now had a flashlight and the ability to make a phone call to Ray for help. Cognitive and memory challenges really suck and can be humiliating and sometimes humorous! Embarrassed, I pulled my phone out of my back pocket, "I didn't realize I had this on me!" I said to my unsuccessful rescuer. "I can call my buddy. He's up on the beach. *He will help us!*"

I turned my cell phone's flashlight on, scanning the area around us. It only revealed blackberry thickets as well as nettle bushes *EVERYWHERE*. As far as we could tell, from the limited light of my phone, there was no way out but through the thicket. And I was definitely not dressed for that.

I clicked on Ray's cell number in my phone contacts. He answered right away. "**CHUCK!** Where are you? I've been worried sick! I didn't even think that you might have your cell phone with you!"

"Ray, listen," I said earnestly. "I'm lost in the woods. I can't get out. Can you come help me?"

"In the woods **where**?!" he demanded. Then he collected himself as he always did and took charge. "Let me figure out where you are. There is a road between the wooded area and the beach. Are you in there?"

"Yes, I think so. I hear cars driving by above me on the gravel road now and then."

"Good," he said in a comforting tone. "I'm going to go get your car. Thank God I have your keys. Now, as soon as I get in the car, I'll call you back. How much charge do you have left on your phone?"

I quickly looked at my phone. "I've got 20% left, Ray. I think it will hold out." My anxiety began fading away. Ray was one of my rocks. I knew beyond a shadow of a doubt that he would get the other guy and me out of there."

"Hang up," Ray said. "It'll take me about ten minutes to get up to your car. **DO NOT MOVE**!!" He commanded me. "Just wait there and trust me. **And don't use the flashlight on your phone!**" He added with an eerie intuition.

"Okay. I'll turn it off now. But someone else is down here too. He came down to try to help, and now he's stuck here with me."

"Tell him help is on the way. Everything is going to be okay," Ray assured me again. "Now hang up and wait for me to call back. DO NOT MOVE from where you are, Chuck! And leave the cell flashlight *OFF!* I need you to have a working phone to find you."

"Okay, thanks, man," my voice trailed off as I realized Ray had hung up and moved into action.

"What did he say?" The guy asked me.

"Ray's coming to get us," I assured him.

"What, how? He'll just get lost too! Or stuck in the thickets!"

"Oh, *NO!*" I assured my fellow captive of the blackberry thickets. "You don't know Ray. He won't give up till he finds us. Trust me."

"Okay," he said, sounding doubtful. I turned my phone's flashlight off as Ray had instructed me. We stood there in the dark for about 10 minutes with me explaining my night blindness and how I got stuck down there. We were both relieved when my cell phone finally rang.

"Chuck," Ray said calmly. "I'm going to drive your car slowly down the gravel road. You stay on the phone with me. I'll honk the horn every 10 seconds. Let me know when I'm getting closer or if I'm going in the wrong direction."

"Okay,… got it," I said.

"Do you hear me honking yet?" Ray asked after a few seconds.

"Um …I think so. Do it again." There it was, clearly. A car horn honked from somewhere above us but down the road. I wondered how far I had wandered into the woods and how much farther I'd gone in trying to find my way out? "Ray, you're getting closer. Keep coming."

"Let me know when you hear the horn right above you."

"Okay… keep coming." I could actually see the headlights of my car shining through the tops of the trees from the road above. "Ray, stop!" I shouted.

"Chuck," Ray then explained to me, "There are a couple of other cars up here that are going to shine their headlights in your direction. I'm going to come to the edge of the road where you can see our car lights. Turn the flashlight of your cell phone on and shine it up in my direction. I've got my machete. I'll come straight down to you." Then he hung up.

Ray to the rescue! I already knew how solution-oriented my best friend was, but this was taking the cake. It was like nothing at all to him to come up with a plan, execute it and accomplish the mission. Ray was one of my heroes, but I soon found out what length this buddy of mine would go to help a friend.

The guy with me and I laughed and joked a bit about the situation now that we were found and soon going to be led out of that dark forest. We heard the thrashing of Ray's machete in the thickets as he made his way down the slope using the flashlight of my cell phone as his guiding light.

I heard Ray shout, "Chuck! I'm about 20 feet away, but you're in the middle of a huge overgrowth of blackberry vines. It's going to take me a few minutes for me to hack away at this and clear a path."

I tried apologizing, "Man, I'm sorry, Ray."

"I got this, Chuck," he cajoled. "You're going to owe me big time!"

It made me feel good that Ray still had his humor through all this. I continued to use my flashlight to guide him. Ray made quite the entrance, thrashing through those last few feet with his handmade machete. He always bragged about how sharp he made them, and at this moment, I was very grateful for his talent and determination and how scary sharp I know his knives and machetes truly are.

As we watched, Ray came through the blackberry thicket. He wore a tank top, jeans, his harness full of tools, a helmet with a headlamp, and a LOT of sweat!

"What happened to you, Chuck?" Ray stared at me with the light of his headlamp shining on me. I looked down for the first time at my chest, feet, and arms. "You have bites *ALL* over you!" he exclaimed.

He was right. But not just mosquito bites. There were welts from the nettles, which were seriously painful. It was difficult to tell the bites from the welts of the nettles.

"Follow me," Ray announced after introducing himself to my fellow rescuee. I took two steps, realizing there was no way I could walk on the thorns.

"Ray, I'm not wearing shoes. Can we walk really slow until we get past the blackberry vines?"

"Get on my back," Ray commanded me. He did not offer; he commanded.

"*NO!* You're not going to carry me out of here, Ray. You've already done enough."

"*Get on my back Chuck.*" I knew that tone. This wasn't up for debate. Ray wasn't much taller than me, maybe an inch or so. Certainly, he had more muscle, but he'd already done enough strenuous work to help get me out of there. I felt he needed a break, and I know there was a part of me that didn't think I was worthy.

"Who does this?" I thought to myself. He was going to have to climb up the hill with me on his back before we got to a path that I could walk on. Yet, I obediently climbed on his back, fighting feelings of humiliation, while the guy with us witnessed this whole ordeal.

With little effort, Ray carried me up the hillside and out of the forest. I marvel at that to this day. Ray never hesitated nor complained; he simply stayed solution-oriented and took care of his friend. I was overwhelmed; I've never had a friend go to such great lengths for me. Ray is certainly one of a kind in my book!

There was also a time when we stopped at a gas station and convenience store to use the restroom. Because it was getting cold, I went to the rear of the car and opened the hatchback to get my jacket. I was closing the hatch when I slammed it down on my head. I have no idea how I managed to do that, but I immediately felt something warm on my head and face. It was running into my eyes, and I was becoming lightheaded.

"Damn it, Ray!" I hollered. "I just cut a gash in my head."

Ray came around the car; without batting an eye, he immediately had me sit down next it on the pavement. "Hold your hand firmly here," he said, pressing my hand flat on the wound.

Ray opened the car door and got his backpack (where he kept his bicycle tools and repair kits). He uses Vaseline to replace tires on his bike when he gets a flat. He grabbed the jar of Vaseline, took a huge swipe of it out of the container, took my hand off my head, and *literally* slapped that goop onto the laceration. "You're **NOT** going to the hospital," Ray said very casually as he put his backpack away. "Just sit here in the front seat. I'll drive. You'll be fine. You have to trust me." So, I did.

There was actually about a two-inch gash at the top of my forehead and about a third of an inch wide. For a week, I kept it clean and did whatever Ray said to care for it. You would never know there had been a huge laceration on my head. There is no scar whatsoever!

I visited Ray often at the camp, helping with any project he was working on at the time, whether it be building a bike from old parts, a new tiny home structure, or remodeling his existing one. As his helper (actually working as a Millwright Helper at a rare metals plant back when I was married), while on a roof or ladder, Ray would ask me for tools (somewhat like a surgeon requesting instruments during an operation). He was always patient when I handed him the wrong tool or couldn't hear his request.

There was something different about being at the camps, the people, the atmosphere. Everyone was what I call *'real,'* living simply and without pretense. I found it to be refreshing and welcoming rather than depressing and oppressive.

Ray, take one more breath.
You can do it …just one more breath Ray …

Ray and I were on an outing to go for a hike at a huge park near the Columbia River in NE Portland late one afternoon. We were in great moods, having a good time as usual. We stopped at a large grocery store to pick up a few items. Ray went inside while I waited in the car. I didn't think he'd be gone long, maybe 10 minutes tops. But Ray seemed to be taking a long time. After about 20 minutes, I called his cell phone. He did not answer. I realized that something wasn't right; I needed to go inside and check on him.

This grocery store was bigger on the inside than it appeared on the outside. I looked down every aisle of that store to find Ray, but he was nowhere to be found. "He must be in the restroom," I thought. That would make the most sense. I saw only two urinals and one stall when I walked into the men's room. I was relieved to see Ray's boots under the stall door. In my good mood, I decided to play one of my impish tricks on him. I took the hat off of my head, tossing it up to the ceiling over the stall. It landed with a plop right next to his boots. But, not one sound or movement came from Ray. "That's not like Ray," I thought to myself

"Ray," I said out loud. No answer. "*Ray!*" I said again but louder. Still no answer. Now I was alarmed. I walked across the restroom to the stall door. "*RAY! You, okay?*" Still, no answer. Fortunately, there was a gap between the door and the latch. I peered inside. To my horror, still barely seated on the toilet, Ray was flopped over on his side, his head nearly touching the floor. I feared he wasn't breathing.

As if I were channeling Ray, I was on autopilot. I got the stall door open and pulled him upright on the commode, putting my ear up to his nose and mouth. I heard a breath after several seconds, but it was very shallow. I kept his head on my shoulder with his mouth and nose up to my ear while I checked his pulse. His breaths were few and far between, but his pulse was strong and steady. I had no idea why Ray passed out.

My mind raced, wondering what to do next. I patted Ray's cheeks, trying to get him to come to, telling him, *"Ray, you gotta wake up!"* Then a guy walked into the restroom. I told him that my friend had blacked out. He wanted to know if an ambulance should be called. I feared Ray's wrath over that suggestion. I told the guy, "I'm not sure. I just found him. I'm trying to get him to wake up."

The guy left, and I continued to hope Ray would come out of it. I'd never been in this situation before. I'd had CPR training countless times over the years while working in healthcare. But this situation was new for me. I went through a gamut of emotions, kneeling there, holding Ray upright, listening to his breaths. I wanted to get angry, cry, and smack him upside the head, yet, hold him steady and keep him alive. I really didn't know what to do other than make sure he was breathing, but those breaths were shallower now and fewer and farther between. I knew it was time to call an ambulance.

That's when, thankfully, an employee finally came into the restroom while I called Ray's name louder and smacked him a little harder on the cheeks. But at first, she accused us of doing *God only knows what*. I got angry at this ignorant accusation and yelled at her, **"You better call for an ambulance because this man is not breathing!"** That changed her tune in a split second; she rushed off to call 911.

When the paramedics arrived, I gave them Ray's information and told them to take him to OHSU, certain they would take the best care of my buddy. I did *not* want to lose him. Ray's parents and I were friends. I chose to call his friend, Ester, first, letting her know he was en route to OHSU by ambulance. I decided to wait to call Ray's parents until I knew more about his situation.

I met the ambulance at the hospital. The staff allowed me to stay with Ray in the ICU after they intubated him. Ray had stopped breathing all together in the ambulance. A nurse kept watch over him while I spoke to Ray, promising that he was going to be okay and that he needed to pull out of this.

"You can do this, Ray! I need my best friend around." Watching someone close to me near death was a whole new life experience. It was hard to fight back the tears, standing next to his bed as a machine breathed for him, keeping him alive. Ray wasn't waking up and not responding to my voice, nor the nurse's. I worked to be strong for Ray's sake. That's what he'd do.

After about an hour, I watched as a team of eight doctors and nurses quietly walked into the room, closing the door behind them and dimming the lights. Instantly I feared they were going to pull the plug. But instead, they formed a circle around Ray's hospital bed. Then softly, one by one, each began talking Ray back to life by gently encouraging him to breathe.

After several requests, with each doctor and nurse, one by one encouraging him to take a breath, they promised him he could go home when he was breathing on his own. They mentioned that I was in the room with him, and I, too, gently spoke to Ray, encouraging him to take a breath. Ray eventually coughed and gagged, struggling to take that first breath on his own. When he finally did, I knew that Ray's determination and will to live were firmly intact. It took much more of the doctor's and nurse's coaxing and coaching, *"Take one more breath, Ray. You can do it, just one more breath..."* to get Ray to take each of his next breaths over what must have been fifteen minutes, possibly more. And eventually, he took another breath, by himself. It was a miracle watching him start to breathe on his own and literally come back to life. I was scared I'd lost my best buddy—a man who had looked out for me and walked with me through some really dark times. Even though, all the while, he was going through very dark times of his own.

Like the births of my daughters, it was one of the most remarkable experiences of my life, watching this team work together to save a man's life by simply being present and encouraging him to live.

Ray took a minute or so to respond to each request made by those doctors and nurses. Knowing Ray as well as I did, he would comply because, even though he was unconscious and not breathing on his own, he *HATED* hospitals. I told the nurses that. They asked me to talk Ray into staying the night after he woke up. I explained to them, "The first thing Ray will want when he wakes up," I laughed, adding, "AND *after* he flirts with the nurse, is ask for his clothes and then to be discharged as soon as he is dressed." I was only forewarning them. Yet, they pleaded with me in hopes that I could talk Ray into staying overnight for observation. I told them I'd give it my best shot but reminded them of the prognosis of his non-compliant response.

Soon Ray was breathing without being coached, and he opened his eyes. Everyone cheered, ***"Good job, Ray!"*** The nurses removed the tube from his throat, telling him to relax as they did so.

With his eyes open, Ray took a look at his nurse and smiled. He immediately turned on the charm. I laughed out loud with tears streaming down my face. *Ray was back!*

"We're leaving right away, Chuck," Ray said after he'd accomplished his task of flirting with a pretty young nurse. I was sure she was charmed, but she never let on. She was a wise woman. I chuckled quietly to myself, knowing Ray's easily predictable behavior.

The nurse spoke to Ray, glancing at me, stating, "Well, your friend and the doctors are hoping you'll agree to stay. Just for the night."

Ray replied with that charming and difficult to resist smile of his, "Well, what did you have in mind?" We all laughed, but without missing a beat, he added, "*I hate hospitals.* I'll be fine. I really gotta go."

I gave the nurse an 'I told you so' look, then turned to Ray, "Just for the night, Ray. Think about it, please." It was a token request just to appease the nurse and doctors. I knew I'd be wasting my breath and risk irritating Ray by pursuing the request any further.

Without responding, Ray looked over at the nurse smiling and asked, "When can I get my clothes?"

"Uh, Ray," I explained gently to him, "The paramedics had to cut all of your clothes off you. But I've got a pair of pants and a shirt in a bag here for you to wear." I could see the wheels turning in Ray's head, trying to recall what he was wearing and, worse, which of his favorite clothes he may have lost. Ray can be quite the dresser, meticulously so. He was soon dressed and ready to leave for my place. It was 2 am by the time he was discharged. But it was a happy Ray that left that hospital and an even happier buddy getting him home safely.

Currently, Ray and his little dog, Isabella, are happily housed in a nice apartment. He spends his time sketching, painting, and hand-making beautiful coffee and end tables from large burls of wood. Yes, the burls are very heavy and are hauled, by Ray, to his home, on his bicycle.

Success was born out of the determination of one of Portland's notorious outcasts. His is a success that is well earned. A story told here, all due to that initial **sidewalk smile.**

> I treasure these adventures with a true friend, the amazing, notorious, unflappable, and my invariably charming buddy, Ray! Oh, and that Norco single-speed bicycle Ray was on when I met him, he sold it to me in 2019 for a great price. I love that bike! *Peace and love to you, my brother… ALWAYS!*
>
> *– Chuck*

By the fall of 2015, I was hopeless and homeless myself, unable to work due to episodes of Post-Traumatic Stress, anxiety, and severe depressive disorders, which led me, once again, into self-medicating. I suppose I could have left Portland to live with relatives in my hometown, but that would mean giving up much-needed medical and mental health resources. So, I chose to live on the streets. A tough decision, but I felt, not only did I have no other choice, but something deep inside me called for me to "let go." If homelessness was to be part of my journey, then so be it. I have no clue what drove me to accept this part of my journey and gave me the courage to do so, but I walked into that darkness boldly and without reservation.

Chapter Three

"Homeless Encounters of the Third Kind: Into the Hearts of the Street Community"

It was late October; my sister Carole came to help me put my belongings into storage. It was a lot of work. Bless her heart! After we finished, she took me to my favorite Chinese restaurant for dinner in the Hollywood District. When we finished enjoying an exceptionally delicious meal, we parted ways. She was in her car heading back to our hometown, and I had my backpack, walking down the sidewalk of NE Broadway, not knowing where I would go or where I would sleep that night. I barely remember trying to curl up underneath a bush next to a church on Sandy Blvd around 1 am. My best effort to keep dry. When the sun came up, I knew I should start moving, it was cold, damp, and I was more uncomfortable than I can remember being my entire life. I don't remember sleeping.

That first week, Portland had one of the worst torrential downpours I'd ever seen. During that downpour, walking alongside Sandy Boulevard towards downtown hoping to get a meal, I had a firsthand experience of how bad one's feet can hurt when having to walk all day trying to avoid being told to move along by business employees and homeowners. But this was nothing compared to the soaking I got from the rain. My shoes filled with water, my backpack grew heavy from all the weight (everything in it completely soaked), let alone the weight of my jacket and clothing, all soaked like a sponge. A sponge that was impossible to wring out. I wondered how and where I would ever get dry. Hopelessness kept a close vigil over me.

Personally, I did not feel I looked homeless, but those that are, we can tell. And in an uncanny way, we have the ability to perceive one another's needs. One morning I was hungry. I usually go to the Blanchet House or a day center to have a meal. It was going to be a couple of hours before a meal would be served anywhere close by. Standing at a bus stop on Sixth Street near Burnside, I heard a voice behind me say, "Here, you need to eat. Have a sandwich." I turned to find a young man sitting on a bench, his hair a mess, as well as his clothing. He was dirty and had scabs on his face and looked to me to be very ill and in need of food and medical attention. He was quietly eating a sandwich and pointed at a bag sitting next to him.

"Dude, I can't take your food. You save that for yourself; you'll want to eat it later when you get hungry."

"No really, take it," he said with a smile. "I know you're hungry. Never refuse a blessing." How can I refuse a heart like that? I sat down next to him on the bench. In the bag was a freshly wrapped Subway sandwich. We quietly ate together. Then he had to take off, "Have a good day, sir," he said with another smile.

This was the moment I learned that those out on the streets are the ones that are the most giving. They know the need firsthand and give out of their own need. This lesson humbled me. So often in my life, I only gave out of my abundance, never out of my own need.

During those months, as I waited for a housing opportunity and disability payments to arrive, Ray, Chris, Gina, Bill, and Nichole all tried to help. But lease agreements only allowed them to let me stay for a couple of weeks. Bill and Nichole helped far more than they should have. My dear friend, Scott, was no longer with us, and I didn't want to be a burden to anyone.

The Journey Begins

In this chapter of my journey into the hearts of the homeless, I met a whole new group of street folk. They are what I call the "untraditionally housed" population. Many of these individuals choose life on the streets. It is their lifestyle and with a completely different stigma attached to it. I was to learn from this part of my journey that there would be a great deal of opposition along the way. In addition to the obvious, it was like an unseen enemy worked to hinder Love's plans for me.

Depression, anxiety, PTSD; these disabilities now looming over my head, as well as a losing battle with addiction, all created havoc in my life along with my homeless experience. Each of these trials had become unwelcome companions and demanded my undivided attention.

This was especially true when I finally approached moving into a downtown apartment building after being homeless for about three months. I was already experiencing the oppression of these disabilities when a whole new genre of oppression reared its ugly head, desiring residency in my mind, wanting to destroy every bit of self-worth and confidence that I once knew.

Grateful to soon be 'inside' (as the homeless call it) and off the streets, I somewhat joyfully went through the lease signing process with the manager. All was well *until*, right after I signed on the dotted line and handed him the check, the manager said, *"There is a group of street kids that hang out on the corner. They are aggressive panhandlers. You are NOT allowed to talk or engage with them!"* He spoke these words in a stern, condescending, and demanding tone with absolutely no eye contact.

In my past, I would have believed every word of this, most likely even walking in the opposite direction or clear around the block to avoid the undesirables. I very likely would have done this for as long as my tenancy lasted. But I wondered about this verbal restriction. It wasn't in the lease. I was also a bit curious about these 'aggressive panhandlers.' Yet, grateful for my new home, I didn't want to 'rock the boat' and didn't challenge the manager's words. But I did think about the street youth I'd met 12 years before. There was nothing aggressive about them at all.

In my 30 years of rental history, I'd never experienced a negative relationship with property managers or my neighbors. Just the opposite, they were mostly all healthy and positive relationships. Even as a homeowner back when I was in my 20's, relationships with my neighbors were nurturing and positive experiences. We looked out for one another.

Unfortunately, and sadly, that was NOT to be the case in this new apartment community. I learned this within the first two weeks. I also took note of a sign in the lobby that curiously read:

"If you see something, say something.
If someone or something appears to be suspicious, say something."

It was signage I'd not seen in any of the buildings I'd lived in before this. I realized, all too soon, this fostered an environment of suspicion, division, and a lack of trust among neighbors. It also hindered a healthy atmosphere within the community.

Residents were constantly in and out of the manager's office all day long complaining about one another with their suspicions and discontent. This was something the manager confided in me during the lease signing process. Now, not only was I dealing with the onset of my disabilities, but that of a crippled (maybe even sabotaged) apartment community; a place that was supposed to be my home and a safe haven.

This oppression became an all-new, confusing, and very real ingredient in the maddening chaos of my world. Within the first two weeks of moving in, one of my neighbors had me written up for being too loud during their sleeping hours, which was daytime since they worked the graveyard shift. The manager firmly rebuked me for having the music too loud (not caring to ask how loud the music really was or if I was even home at the time, which I wasn't). Rather arrogantly, he commanded me, "You will need to buy headphones to listen to music during the day. Good headphones will only cost you about $80!"

This neighbor also came to my door one afternoon, telling me he'd got the tenant living in my apartment before me and the one before that kicked out. ***"AND I'M GOING TO GET YOU KICKED OUT TOO!"*** he yelled at me, for all the neighbors down the hall to hear.

I shut the door in tears, wondering what the world was coming to. This studio apartment I'd been so excited to move into was not a 'home;' it was becoming a prison.

Ishaan and the Dancing Girl: Blessing the Journey

I don't know that I've ever felt so alone in my entire life than I did after signing that lease. My only possessions when I moved in were a backpack, a change of clothes, some toiletries, and a blanket. Even though I was now inside, there was an unexpected and alarming sadness enveloping and overwhelming me, the darkness within me stealing my energy, appetite, and will to live.

Within the first few days, I realized the darkness was rapidly closing in on me. It was on a Saturday morning that, in desperation, all I could think of to do was reach out to my ever-supportive friends on a social network. I simply asked for prayer.

Later that evening, I forced myself to leave the false security of isolation, traveling on foot through the heart of downtown to get myself something for dinner, yet there was not a food I could think of that appealed to me, nor even stirred my appetite. I couldn't afford to lose any more weight than I already had. Not only was my appetite gone, but so was my connection to my heart and my ability to find hope.

The Saturday evening nightlife had already begun. Neither the hustle and bustle of downtown Portland's nightlife nor the street drummers and aromas from the local food carts and the winter decorations and lights hanging from the trees and lampposts were affecting my mood, nor my appetite even a tiny bit on that walk. I felt oddly alone in a sea of people. I purchased a frozen pizza at the grocers. I began the emotionally arduous journey back to my new home, dreading having to return there and fearing that all too familiar fall I often take deep into despair and a self-inflicted, or self-induced, isolation.

During that walk, I realized that all these feelings of emptiness, darkness, and loneliness tell me one VERY important thing; that even though I felt broken and empty, I have a heart. I may only feel pain today. But I *do* have a heart, for which I am grateful.

At that moment, I noticed two people on the street corner ahead of me. There was a well-dressed young couple who appeared to be trying to connect with each passer-by. With a beautiful all-American girl-next-door look about her, the young woman held a small stuffed Orca whale in her hand that she playfully used as a puppet. The young man was tall, slender, and dark-skinned. The two of them were far too happy for my mood, and, like the others passing by, I planned to give them the cold shoulder. The thought of someone I don't know attempting to make me smile and be happy, annoyed me.

As I tried to move past them unnoticed, the young man turned to me with a broad, beautiful smile. Looking directly into my eyes, he happily proclaimed, in a melodic East Indian accent, *"I think we should meet."*

For some unexpected reason, he spoke to a place deep in my heart. It did not change my mood, but it did offer me a break from the loneliness.

The young woman began to softly sing or hum an unrecognizable, yet lovely melody. She and the little stuffed Orca in her hand began joyfully dancing around the two of us. I looked up into his eyes and offered the young man my hand stating, "My name is Chuck."

With a smile and his warm hand in mine, he asked, "Ah, is that short for Charles?"

"Yes, do you know the meaning of Charles?" I asked him as I found myself beginning to ignore my somber mood.

With sincere interest and eye contact completely engaged, he said, "No, I do not. But what is the meaning?"

As the words left my lips, I wondered how true they were in my current weakened state, "It means strong, manly, man of [Love]," I answered him, nearly hesitating. Then asked him, "And what is your name?" I was beginning to consider offering him a smile.

In his beautifully melodic accent, he stated, "*Ishaan.*"

"What is the meaning of Ishaan?" I asked, feeling a bit more comfortable with the situation. He explained that it had to do with a constellation of stars, Taurus, to be specific. He then added with a smile, "But I was born in December." We both chuckled.

Ishaan then asked me, "What do you do?"

With sadness gripping me at that moment, due to the reminder of my life's work lost, I stated, "I do social work normally, but currently I volunteer at homeless camps." I surprised myself with what I said next. "I've had a dark and depressing week," I admitted to Ishaan. "I've been unable to find hope in my current circumstances. I'm unable to work. It appears I have some disabilities. I've felt very alone and isolated. But *you*, Ishaan, have helped to brighten my day. You have offered me a glimmer of light. I don't feel so alone now."

"May I give you a hug?" Ishaan offered with a beautiful, compassionate smile and his arms outstretched wide.

"Yes, please," I answered, wrapping my arms around him as he tightly wrapped his around me. We embraced like old friends, and the young woman stopped singing and dancing. Then with the most delightful smile one could ever imagine, she wrapped her arms around the both of us.

This loving triune hug was unimaginable in my despair just minutes before. I bid them a fond farewell as I parted ways with them. It made my heart sad to leave my two new friends; their lights shone brightly for this old guy that evening. Yet, when I left them, I did so with a hopeful smile returning to my face.

To this day, I honestly believe they bestowed a blessing upon me. A blessing for the journey I was soon, unknowingly, about to take into the hearts of the street community. Sometimes I wonder if they were angels. Maybe they were, maybe not. But I will treasure them in my heart always. For the darkness within me, albeit only a bit of it, had been replaced in those moments by those two precious souls sharing themselves and their hearts with me on the sidewalks of downtown Portland, one lonely and hopeless winter evening, that was beautifully interrupted by love.

The so-called "aggressive" panhandlers & Dirty Jeff

I suppose it was curiosity that gave me the courage to disobey that stern warning my apartment manager gave me after signing the lease. Heading out of my apartment building to run a few errands one afternoon, I noticed a few people chatting up ahead on the corner. As I casually approached them, I found several fascinating characters. They were each dressed in unusual street attire made of canvas and leather with interesting patches and holes that seemed to be strategically placed here and there on their clothing. Some sported dreadlocks, mohawks, or wore bandanas around their heads. "Those *aggressive panhandlers!*" I thought to myself. In my mind, these were the forbidden outcasts. I didn't want to startle or aggravate the group, but I only thought this due to the manager's judgmental perspective regarding the homeless.

Jeff (affectionately called Dirty Jeff) immediately connected with me simply through eye contact, his eyes noticeably blue. He was tall with dark curly hair and wore a red handkerchief on top of his head. He is a handsome young man for certain. "How you doin' man?" he asked, with a dimpled grin and an unlit cigarette hanging from his mouth as I passed by.

"I'm okay," I said, wondering about these young folk and why they all seemed to be so happy, even carefree.

"I'm Jeff," he said with a nod as he lit the cigarette.

"I'm Chuck," I said, thinking to myself, "not that it matters." I wasn't supposed to even acknowledge this group. But I pursued the conversation anyway. Jeff had taken the time to introduce himself. That spoke volumes in this old guy's world. "Thanks for saying hey, Jeff. I'm learning that this neighborhood is sometimes not so friendly."

"*BOY HOWDY!*" Jeff said, almost laughing, glancing up at the apartment building. "How long have you lived downtown?"

"It's been just a few weeks. I live upstairs," giving that same *knowing* glance upward that Jeff did. This made us both chuckle. Then Jeff introduced me to his buddies. I only remember Hollywood and Ricky, but there were a few others as well. Surprisingly, I felt comfortable with these guys, and not one of them asked me for a dime.

After the introductions, I parted ways with them, hoping to chat with Jeff again and possibly the others. It was a refreshing encounter. Far different than my experiences with the manager and my neighbor.

Within two weeks, my buddy Chris and his wife Gina came to my rescue. From their storage unit, Chris brought a maple dinette table with two matching chairs, an antique secretary's desk, a modern-looking pleather and chrome swivel recliner, and a vintage 7-foot-long 1970s console stereo with a turntable and cassette player. It was all in perfect working order, and the cabinet was in great condition. I was blown away. Here my old street buddy was repaying me with the same kindness that I had offered him about ten years earlier.

Through meeting Jeff and his buddies, the generosity of old friends, and a nearly furnished apartment, depression would be barking up the wrong tree with this old guy. But still, I wasn't convinced I had the strength to battle it alone.

It wasn't long before I invited Jeff up to my place to shower, a brief hiatus from the streets. He sometimes played his favorite music for me, a genre I was unfamiliar with. It was some sort of blend with American Folk. I liked it, but mostly I liked that Jeff wanted to share his interests with me. He was becoming a good friend. I would confide in him about feeling uncomfortable with living in the building, noting the manager's warning and my neighbor's promise to get me kicked out. I think Jeff thought I was exaggerating. But at least he quietly listened as a good friend would.

He never said anything, but I knew Jeff hung out with me because he sensed my depression and loneliness. It was not that he felt sorry for me; as I look back, I realize Jeff is a very strong empath. Jeff's presence and friendship, along with his friends' cheerful greetings every day, were helping to breathe life back into this old guy as well as providing me with a sense of community and feeling safe. At the time, Jeff was just 22 years old.

I remember an afternoon shortly after Jeff started hanging out with me. We were in the kitchen, sitting at the table chatting. There came a knock on my door. It's a secure building, so I wondered who the heck it could be? When I opened the door, it revealed the presence of my neighbor, the one I dreaded. He was there to continue his hatefully aggressive work at getting me evicted. Jeff got to see the oppression I was living under firsthand.

Without going into a lot of dialogue, the neighbor offered no response to my greeting. He loudly complained about the "noise coming from my apartment" and the smell of cigarettes (I don't smoke and don't allow smoking in my apartment). He complained about other odd things as well. Then he turned his face away, looking down the long hallway, he shouted, *"...AND EVERYONE KNOWS YOU'RE A DRUG ADDICT!"*

I was speechless, embarrassed, and weakened by his hatefulness. I simply said, "Thank you for letting me know about your concerns." Now in despair, I quietly shut the door.

"Wow, Chuck!" Jeff admitted. "You were right about that guy. He's a jerk!" Jeff knew just how to comfort me and hung out the rest of the afternoon. He was slowly becoming one of my rocks. Not only that, but I began to see him as a gift.

I fear Jeff received the brunt of my fears due to so much oppression in that apartment building. One Monday morning after he'd spent the night, he showered and spent a great deal of time dressing himself, getting his street attire and Dirty Kid accessories just right. It was kinda fun watching him get ready for the outside world. I'd not realized that it was such an event, pulling that 'look' together.

The evening before, I gave Jeff a pair of new jeans that didn't fit me. I hoped that he would wear them when he left the building that morning. I didn't want the management to identify him as one of the so-called *aggressive panhandlers*. I would most certainly find myself in trouble once again. I became very anxious, remembering that stern warning after I signed the lease. Those kids being aggressive panhandlers was certainly one perspective, but my heart challenged those verbal *rules*, and none of what the manager said, in my experience, was ever true. It was contrived and fear-based. It was the manager, employees, and many of the residents that were clearly the aggressors.

So, as Jeff got ready to leave, even though I thought Jeff looked really cool, I was nervous about what the neighbors might think and told him so. "Jeff, at least change your pants, please," I begged him. He wore his favorite jeans decorated with the usual holes and patches. With a look of disappointment, he quietly said, "But this is what I want to wear."

Knowing Jeff had witnessed me get chastised by a neighbor firsthand and verbally warned about other ridiculous issues, I begged him to at least change his tattered and patched-up jeans into the new pair I'd given him. He seemed hurt, and I knew he felt judged. He respectfully repeated, "But this is what I want to wear."

I got upset, so fearful that I would get evicted, I lashed out at him. I kept repeating, "I'm going to get kicked out! I'm going to get kicked out! How can you do this to me?" In my fear, I was freaking out.

I know I was rude, hurtful, and thoughtless, even downright mean. I remember our ride downstairs in the elevator; Jeff was sad. As hard as I worked to love these kids, I let the oppression I lived under lead me to be the oppressor.

I ask myself now, which is of greater value, being hurtful and oppressive or being kind and understanding? To simply trust that no matter how Jeff is dressed, that Love will cover me for having spent time with him and getting to know him better. I had some good quality time with my buddy and had now replaced that quality time with judgment and scorn. I've had a lot of regrets about that incident, but I learned something; I definitely learned something. I learned that what the world sees as wrong is not what Love sees as right. What is truly *right versus wrong*? Doing that which is judgmental and hurtful or doing what is right through the eyes of Love? I've learned the hard way to work to choose the way of Love. Social norms can often suck!

In the summer of 2018, I ran into Jeff a couple of blocks from my old apartment on Third. A year before, I moved out to NE Portland. But now, I was living in a shelter program downtown. My housemate, Doug, and I had been displaced by a fire. Jeff's dimpled greeting and that unique way he said, "Chuuuuck," got my attention right away. It was so good to see my old buddy once again. We slowly walked together up Third. We ended up standing in the very same spot where I met Jeff.

"Remember that book I said I wanted to write about meeting all you guys and our adventures? About all the love you guys gave me?" Jeff nodded at me, glancing up from his tedious task, rolling a cigarette. "Well, I need some photos for that book. Is it okay if I take a few now?"

"Suuure." Came Jeff's reply. This old guy was not surprised at Jeff's unique delivery of that simple word. I began snapping photos of him with my phone. He sat on a ledge running along the north side of the building and around each of the corners to the east and west. This was the perfect setting to get some photos of Jeff. The beauty of it was that this was completely unplanned.

Jeff asked to see the pics when I was done. He chuckled at a few, then snapped some shots of himself. I wasn't surprised. He switched it to selfie mode and began adjusting his scarf, surveying the unique landscape of his street kid look. He really is a handsome guy. He doesn't let on, but he knows it. It's important to mention that the photo the editors and I chose (to photoshop into the sketched image) for this segment is one that Jeff snapped of himself with my phone that day. The dude's got talent! I asked Jeff if he considered himself a Dirty Kid. He gave me a serious look, "I consider myself an artist. I write songs and some other things."

Learning this made me hope he'd share his talents. "I'd love to see your work someday."

"I don't have anything right now," he said. "But I can work on something."

It was great catching up with Jeff and reminiscing. I felt it was important that he knew how much I appreciated him and his friendship. "Jeff, you need to know something. I don't know if you realize it, but you helped me through a very dark time in my life when we met." I kinda choked up here. "We never talked about it, but I was in a deep depression when we met. You hung out with me and helped me not feel alone. You introduced me to your friends. And put up with my B.S. Who does that, Jeff? You're a really special guy." With that said, Jeff's gaze fell to the ground.

He softly said, "You helped me too."

Suddenly a building employee came by telling us to get away from the building. We were not welcome there. "You scum bags, get lost!" he shouted at us. Jeff is used to this treatment. I am not. Righteous anger boiled within me. I am heartbroken over the abusive treatment the homeless population often experiences. That building employee can verbally abuse us and chase us off. But he can't take the love we shared away.

Fast forward to the summer of 2020. Jeff and his gal Litebulb stayed at my place for a few days. Somehow the mention of my missions to Africa came up in conversation. Jeff's eyes lit up! "You've been to Africa?!" he was more excited than I'd ever seen Jeff before.

"Well, yeah, a couple of times," I said, clarifying why I was there. "I worked in orphanages."

Jeff's excitement grew. "Dude! That's what I've always wanted to do! A mission to Africa!"

This surprised the "hell" right out of me. "The children there are abandoned due to their parents dying of AIDS," I explained to Jeff. "Most of them are hopeless and don't know love. They just want to be loved."

"Wow!" Jeff responded with total sincerity. "I love kids."

"We hang out with them, hold the younger ones for hours, and play soccer with the older ones. It's a blast!"

"If you ever go on another trip to Africa, I would go with you in a heartbeat." Jeff's words were like music to my ears.

"Okay," I said, then filled him in on the dynamics of the trip. "We might be going with an organization called, 'Show Mercy International.' There is a Christian influence, but they are true Believers. They believe in Love. They desire people to be awakened to Love through the journey. How would you feel about that?"

Jeff smiled. "That's not an issue for me." At that moment, I wondered about his background. Was there a faith-based background hidden somewhere in his mysterious life?

"Well then," I promised him. "Plan to have your whole world change. You won't return the same person you were before you left. I plan to go back in the next couple of years. I'll hit you up. YOU'RE GOING WITH ME!"

"AWESOME!" Jeff shot back at me. "Just let me know when."

That conversation ended with me reeling from a new joy and a greater appreciation for my street buddy. I never saw this conversation coming, but boy, am I delighted it did!

You'll find that Dirty Jeff shows up many times throughout these stories. A charming young man, I always give him a shout-out anytime I see him. Jeff's not a hugger, but that dimpled smile is enough of a hug for me.

As time passed and I neared completion of the manuscript, I got stuck. Memories of my brief history on the streets and even in my forties sowing wild oats, bar and club hopping, experimenting with drugs, and bouncing from relationship to relationship, those memories kindled doubt and unworthiness within me. It caused me to question the relationships I've built with some of those on the streets. Thoughts crippling me with the pointed question, "Were those relationships based on a hidden agenda, or were they based on truth and love?" The insidious realm of fraud syndrome often stalked me and worked to derail my heart and my purpose.

Then along comes Dirty Jeff with his strong empathic abilities and caring heart. It was a Thursday evening in mid-summer 2020, maybe three weeks before this manuscript was completed. I found myself receiving a message from Love that I so desperately, yet unknowingly, needed to hear. Never could there have been a more perfect heart for me to hear it from than one of the first kids that welcomed me into the hearts of the street community while I was in one of the darkest depressions of my life.

Jeff, Litebulb, and I were sitting in my apartment that Thursday evening. He and Litebulb had just been through a heartbreaking experience and needed a temporary safe place inside. Litebulb had just been released from the hospital.

"I'm stuck, you guys," I admitted to them. "I can't seem to move forward with the book right now." I did not say why because I feared judgment, as I often do.

Jeff's eyes lit up, leaning forward, looking me squarely in the eye (without knowing any of my dark thoughts and doubts), but with a caring heart and fatherly look of concern, he said boldly, *"Chuck, don't you ever doubt the good you've done for us and others on the street. You've cared for us. You provided a safe place for us to be inside where we were safe, could rest, and get cleaned up. Sure, there were times when some of the kids had or did drugs, but they would have done that anyways out on the streets. Your place was a safe place out of the weather and danger [predators or thieves] when all we had were our sleeping bags out there in the cold and the rain. You've done nothing but good, Chuck. You need to believe that and **never doubt it!**"*

Tears rolled down my cheeks even before Jeff finished. "How did you know Jeff?" I burst out through tears. "I've never told anyone that I've had those doubts. Wow, Jeff, you are definitely a strong empath!"

I stood up, not knowing what to do, how to process this 'word of knowledge' given to Jeff from Love for this self-doubting old guy. I was trying to collect myself to keep from sobbing. Jeff turned to Litebulb; she was resting on the lower bunk of my bed, where the two of them slept during their stay in my tiny studio apartment.

In a whisper, he asked her, "Is he kidding? Is he just making that up?" Jeff was even doubting himself at that moment.

Litebulb turned to Jeff contradicting his doubt, "Jeff, he's not faking. Those are real tears." Shaking off his disbelief and doubts in himself, Jeff got up from his chair and walked across the room towards me, saying, "Chuck come here. You need a big hug."

"Whoa, Jeff," I said, attempting to sound strong. "I know you don't like to hug; you don't have to do …. tha ……"

Jeff stopped me right there, "No, Chuck! You're getting a big hug. I love you." Wrapping me in his arms, Jeff's hug did nothing to diminish the flow of my tears; in fact, it perpetuated the need and joy in releasing them.

Jeff is probably 6 feet 2 inches tall, lanky but strong. He gave me a huge brotherly hug. Even though I am, Jeff is not a hugger, but he pushed himself past his hugging issues to comfort and love this old guy. And that was the beginning of completing this book project. It was probably the first time in the four years we've known one another that Jeff and I have hugged.

Through this unexpected lightbulb moment, Love reminded me that my enlightened experiences *are real*. That the hearts of the street community truly love as I'd discovered and that my heart and my intentions have been a positive thing in helping others in need.

The morning I finished writing and proofing this segment on Jeff, Maxine (his mom whom I'd just met a week prior contacted me through a social network), sent me an email with a document attached. As I read her words, walking home from the gym, tears rolled down my cheeks. I was hearing a mother's heart for her son and the beauty she sees within him.

The Gift of Jeff

"Jeff arrived as a gift to us at the age of three. We had been praying and praying for a child, and God knew exactly what we needed and also what Jeff needed.

He was super curious, very bright, and tall! We called him Chad because that was his birth name, and he had enough changes in his life. We certainly didn't want to continue to confuse him about his own identity.

[Chad's adoptive father's name is Jeff. Chad chose to be called Jeff, like his dad, at a young age.]

He had lots of parties given by family and friends to welcome him. It was a glorious time! We couldn't have been prouder. And our large extended family was especially happy to have this special little boy in their fold.

Jeff was such a fast learner. His favorite thing was having books read to him, or was that mine? He learned to read rather easily as well and became a voracious reader. Instead of toys as treats for good behavior, it was books.

Jeff also loved adventure and went through Cub Scouts and several years of Boy Scouts. Camping, hiking, biking, and white-water rafting were great times outdoors, not only for him but for me as his mom, as well! He also loved the beach and still does. As a little kid, he would build sandcastles and just run around them in circles, continually expelling his energy. He was totally happy swimming and enjoying all the beach activities.

Jeff also considered himself a 'foodie' as he grew into his teenage years. He took some interest in the kitchen as his stepdad and I would cook. We would try to teach certain vital skills we knew would be needed once he left home. His favorite thing to do was grill out. But his favorite meal at home was oxtail stew. We would ask the boys what they wanted to eat, and it was always oxtail stew, which was basically an all-day affair where they would be involved. He even took culinary arts in high school to gain basic knowledge of kitchen skills should he get a job at a restaurant.

What I know about the person Jeff has become showed up in his early teens. He liked going to church and volunteering. One year, our state was hit extremely hard by tornadoes causing extensive damage statewide. Jeff didn't have a job at the time, but I suggested he go to a church, a drop-off point for supplies and help for the tornado victims. And he did. He helped with debris clearing and cleaning up.

The highlight for him was finding and befriending a dog amid the chaos. The help he participated in, I believe, sparked a flame to help others as his heart grew so big for the hurting and the underdog that he always felt he himself was.

Jeff has grown into a loving and caring young man. I believe angels are encamped about him at all times, and he is blessed beyond measure. I do not know where the path he has chosen will take him. I've always known that God has a plan for his life and is using his place in life to reach, teach, and serve us all that know Jeff, and have been [touched] by having him in each of our lives."

"Thank you, Poppa Chuck, for using your experiences and following your heart for this project. You never know how God will use you if you're a willing vessel. You are a blessing to all who know you."

-Max ("Dirty Jeff's" Mom)

"I love you, Jeff! Never doubt that! Thank you for being there for me through one of the darkest times of my life. Your big heart shines bright in this dim world. Keep smiling, my young friend... dimples rule, and you rock handsome! But, more importantly .... your heart rocks Love."

~Poppa Chuuuuck

These kids are not 'just' panhandlers and drifters, as much of our society unknowingly believes (and what I was taught growing up). They are loving, gentle, insightful, sensitive, and talented characters who bring light to this world. A light that the world cannot comprehend and will not see, nor understand, until our eyes are opened to simply 'love,' without judging.

Meeting Jeff is only the beginning of this journey into the hearts of the street community. My whole world was on the edge of being busted wide open with love expanding out of what was like a dark portal. And that it did, on a lonely night when Love began singing me songs of hope from out of the darkness itself.

Chapter Four

"The 'Ledge' of Love":
The Infamous Corner on Third

Peter's Song

I walked along the ledge one dark, cold, and lonely night. It was about 2 am. I really didn't feel like I cared to live or even take another breath. Hopelessness burdened me to the point of insomnia. The emptiness and despair within me were much like falling into a bottomless pit but never hitting bottom. Just falling endlessly, scared of the impending painful splat, longing desperately for death to relieve my pain.

At the corner of the building, I sat down on the ledge, wondering if jumping from it would be like falling into that bottomless pit. "But dang," I thought to myself, "That ledge is only two feet above the sidewalk. I wouldn't even experience a fall or a splat. I'd just have a different spot to sit my old butt on and continue my painful self-absorbed and unfulfilling relationship with emptiness." This was the very spot where I first met Jeff, Ricky, and Hollywood. I sat wondering where they might be and how they were. I hated being alone.

Just then, a figure seated on the ledge just around the corner of the building, about five feet away, scooted toward me, stopping next to me. This seemed to be very odd, especially at this time of night, and should have been unsettling, but for some reason, I felt no fear.

From that figure, or person (I was fairly certain of that) came a cheerful voice quietly asking, "Can I sing you a song?"

I squinted, attempting to adjust my eyes to the darkness and trying to wrap my brain around what was happening. I noticed this person had something large with him. It was on his back. I looked around, thinking he must be speaking to someone else. There was no one else around.

"Sing for *me*? *Why*?" I whispered. I was now able to make out a pleasant-looking guy, probably in his 30s, smiling at me. On his back was a guitar.

"Because I know that you will enjoy and appreciate it," he replied quietly.

"But, it's, it's, two in the morning," I whispered in a stutter. I was reluctant, for I know my neighbors up inside the building. They don't take kindly to street performers singing at night or anywhere near the building, for that matter.

"It's okay, man," he said. "I'll be quiet. My name's Peter; what's yours?" his smile hadn't faded; it brought a forgotten smile to my own face.

"I'm Chuck," I answered, wondering what was about to happen next—wondering if my anxiety would kick in while he sang, with me still fearing the wrath of my neighbors.

"I'm going to sing you a Bob Dylan song." With that, Peter pulled his guitar from his back and began to lightly strum. The words Peter sang to me bewilder me to this day. How did he know?

The heart of that song was about a lonely and lost soul that had given up hope, discouraged by the darkness insidiously closing in on him.

Tears stung my eyes while Peter sang. He looked up from his guitar and into my eyes now and then. Somehow, he knew I needed this song. He knew that the song would reveal to me that I wasn't alone. The song was "Not Dark Yet."

"Not Dark Yet" / Callum Scott

https://youtu.be/lKqhPnn4r5A

Peter sang two more Bob Dylan songs. His voice was beautiful, and his instrumental was flawless. His connection to Love was divinely inspiring. The last song Peter sang was one he had written himself. That one was the clincher. It was beautiful, raw, and real. Peter sang it far better (if that were possible) than he had the others. I do not remember the lyrics, just Peter's heart creating a beautiful and safe space on that ledge where hope began to whisper in my ear, "It's not dark yet."

When he finished, he looked satisfied and happy. Like what he had just done was what he was meant for in those moments with some old guy in the dead of night in downtown Portland.

"Dude, you're very talented," I said. "Thank you for singing for me. Please don't ever stop singing for people. You have a gift. It touches people's hearts." I then added, "I came out here tonight because of depression and loneliness. And because I couldn't sleep. What you've done for me filled a void and has given me hope." Peter hugged me, saying he hoped to see me again one day. I hoped so too. I then went back upstairs, no longer feeling alone, knowing I was truly loved. A shift was beginning to take place in my small embattled world. That ledge was introducing me to a journey I'd never imagined.

Ishaan, that beautiful dancing young woman, and her little Orca puppet, along with Dirty Jeff and now Peter with his songs, helped me to open my mind and heart to a world on the sidewalks and ledges where I was to learn almost anything can happen. But even more so, that love can be found in the most unlikely places—these places forbidden by a harsh, judgmental world where the outcasts long to be seen and heard.

Joseph: Beautifully Broken

Joseph befriended me in the summer of 2016 with an impromptu street performance he offered me and a few others sitting on the ledge at that *Infamous corner on Third* (as the police so endearingly call it). He gave us what was more like a personal concert. Joseph makes his way around downtown by wheelchair, belting out songs that would bring envy to nearly any accomplished vocalist. He also writes songs, some about drugs, alcohol, and life with addiction. Joseph is my friend. He was just 27 years of age at the time.

A lovely young woman named Leslie, who enjoys hanging with Dirty Kids and buskers, is often Joseph's backup singer and duet partner. Buskers are street performers who sing or perform for cash. During that first performance with Joseph, Leslie kept her eye on me during each and every song. Leslie's smile was tethered to my heart, telling me she knew that their songs and their music were touching me deeply, helping to push aside the emptiness within me, and replacing it with their love for music and performing.

As I sat on the ledge outside my apartment building one afternoon, Joseph came rolling around the corner in his wheelchair, looking haggard, sad, and broken. He parked directly in front of me, then anxiously explained his wallet and backpack had been stolen, and his bank account was cleaned out.

"I want to sing a song for you, Chuck," Joseph told me.

I was in awe that in his own distress, Joseph would want to sing for me. "Always," was my reply. But with compassion, I added, "How can you sing me a song when you are feeling like this? You don't have to sing for me right now."

"I really want to," he replied. "It will help me."

"Okay." I agreed but was still concerned for my buddy. He pulled his guitar from the back of his wheelchair and prepared to bless me and those present with his talents, but all the while with an aching heart.

The raw pain coming from Joseph's soul as he sang from the depths of his heart broke mine. He sang for me, for his pain, and for relief from his burdens as long as he could. Until unexpectedly, one of his guitar strings broke. And at that moment, Joseph broke. The tears flowed. All I could offer him were my own tears and my arms to hold him while his body quaked from the emotion and the pain of his suffering, suffering that began long before his wallet and backpack were stolen. You see, at the age of 23, Joseph lost his right leg just below the knee to a rare disease. Now homeless, his personal belongings and prosthetic stolen, with all his loss, fighting his demons, and navigating perpetual hopelessness, Joseph's heart, his spirit, and his love for others were beautifully intact.

One evening that same summer, I went for a walk to keep my head above the murky waters of despair and depression. I wore one of my AIDS Walk t-shirts; the annual event raises funds for a local non-profit that helps individuals living with HIV/AIDS and works to help fight the stigma surrounding the disease.

I was already feeling a hint of warmth stirring my heart after watching "Warm Bodies," a film about zombies that are brought back to life by love. Oh, how I could relate to those Zombies! Never did they think it would be possible to come back to life. But they did. I was grateful for the film and its message, offering me a bit of hope. But even more grateful to unexpectedly run into Joseph beautifying the neighborhood with song, his amazing smile, and infectious laughter.

"Hey, Joseph!" I hollered, waving at him.

Joseph whirled around in his wheelchair, studied my t-shirt, and cried out, *"I walk?! How can you be so insensitive?! Do I look like I can walk?!"* he was pointing down at the stump that was all that remained of his right leg.

My heart sank for a split second as I looked down to see that my t-shirt simply read, "I WALK" in BIG BOLD, red and white letters, on a navy-blue background. I was mortified!

Then Joseph began to chuckle and tell his stories of living in San Francisco and terrorizing the AIDS Walk volunteers with his *"How dare you, I can't walk"* routine during the AIDS Walk season. He got a laugh out of me as I pictured some of my SF buddies experiencing Joseph's playful sense of humor firsthand. Then Joseph cried out, "I would sooo wear that shirt!"

"Seriously, Joseph? You want my shirt?"

Delighted, he proclaimed, "Oh yeah!"

I ran up to my room, changed, and brought Joseph's new prized shirt to him. He couldn't get his t-shirt off fast enough. His friends loved the whole ordeal, and a nearby cop nodded his head with approval which is a rare occurrence at that infamous corner on Third.

One of my favorite stories about Joseph came after an evening when all hell broke loose at the ledge.

Louie's Makeshift Street Band

It was around dusk; I was out for a walk on the waterfront and heading back home on Third when I came across Louie sitting on the ledge working on his guitar. He always seemed to be a bit of a loner and a very serious young man. But he can play the guitar and sing beautifully—one of the many things I admire about him.

I wondered if he would be performing sometime that evening. I didn't want to interrupt his work and have always been a bit intimidated by him. I was going to quietly stroll on by, but Louie looked up from his guitar, humbly asking, "Do you have any tools? I need to fix my guitar." My memory doesn't serve me here, I don't remember having any tools, but I do remember sitting on the ledge while Louie was hard at work.

As time went on, we were joined by more of the gang; Leslie, Hollywood, Scooby, and Ricky, to name a few. It was cool hanging out with these young folks, so unpretentious and full of life, and always welcoming me into their world.

Everyone was having a good time. This was a real community coming together with joy, fun, love, and laughter, embracing everyone present. All was well until a resident (and employee) of the apartment building came stumbling up to us. He was drunk and demanded that my friends leave the area.

"You guys are TRASH, SCUM!!" he shouted at the kids. "You don't belong here! Get lost!" Then for no apparent reason, he threatened to punch Scooby, even drawing back his fist. I was shocked and horrified then found myself jumping into action.

Not that Scooby needed me to, instinctively (which is something I'd done maybe only once before in my life). I jumped between the two. Facing my neighbor, I folded my arms across my chest. Calmly and firmly, I stated, "These are my friends. If you're going to hit someone, you'll have to go through me."

Oddly, at that moment, he stumbled backward and landed on his ass. Then got up and scurried off like a scared rat. To me, it was like a giant invisible hand grabbed him by the shirt, pushed him back a step, then sat him on the ground. We all looked at one another, echoing, "What the heck just happened?" It was like Love had intervened in a profound and powerful way.

My friends thanked me for caring for them, which I hadn't expected nor truly understood the depth of at that time. "Does this happen often, Scooby?" I asked.

"Every day," came Scooby's reply.

My heart broke, and I had to ask myself, "Hearts that need love and understanding the most, treated as outcasts, taunted and ridiculed, what kind of world is that?"

It seemed only moments had gone by, and Louie was back at work. To my delight, he was preparing to entertain everyone on the sidewalk that evening.

"Chuck, do you have a five-gallon bucket and possibly a broom you don't need?" Louie asked.

"I actually have two brooms (for whatever reason, but now it was obvious). You can have one of them, and I have a clean bucket from Voodoo Donuts. I'll get both of them and be right back," I assured him. I couldn't wait to get back downstairs from my apartment with a broom and the bucket. I had no idea what he wanted them for, but I was excited and intrigued.

"These are perfect. Thank you," he said, taking them into his care. It was like Louie was on autopilot and had done this hundreds of times before.

"What are you using them for?" I asked him.

"I'm going to make a bass. You'll see," he said, continuing with his task. Louie turned the five-gallon bucket upside down. I watched him use his knife to cut a hole about the size of the broom handle into the bottom. Just then, his hand slipped. I was horrified to see blood running down his leg. He didn't appear to notice and kept on working.

With concern, I said, "Dude, do you need any bandages? It looks pretty bad."

"I need to finish this first," he said, not looking up from his work. Louie's task was more important to him at that moment than caring for himself. This young man is driven by his love for music and busking. Within seconds, he had the hole secured in the bottom of the bucket. Looking at his leg, he said, "I've gotta take care of this. I don't want to expose anyone to the blood." This impressed me. He is very aware of the need for safety in this day and age (regardless of anyone's blood-borne disease status) *and* that he cared. That was the moment where the father-heart within me broke for this young man. I was moved by his concern, more for the safety of others and to entertain them than for himself.

As Louie cleaned up the gash on his leg, covering it with a good patching of bandages, the development of his street band continued. He unscrewed the broom handle, discarding the head, then stuck the broomstick in the hole; I'm not sure how he secured it there. I was enjoying the distraction of more of our street buddies entering the scene; they all began supporting and encouraging Louie as well.

It wasn't long before he attached a string somehow at the bottom of the bucket, running it up the broomstick; a bass! I could see it now. Leslie was nearby, excited to soon play the instrument Louie was creating for her.

Moments later, they began harmonizing with Orion playing an antique washboard, Louie with his banjo, and Leslie took her place on the bass. From the long line at Voodoo Donut, patrons brought quarts of milk along with donuts for this hungry group. Along with smiles of appreciation, they were placed on the sidewalk next to the open banjo case. I was amazed at the community that appeared around me. I simply sat and loved these guys, hoping all the while to hear more of their stories and songs. They sang their hearts out that evening and have held a special place in my heart ever since.

Louie Laveine and The Last Circus / **Just Left Town**

https://youtu.be/dehYv602VWE

While the band played on, Ricky shared with me, through tears, how he dearly missed his thirteen-year-old son and seven-year-old daughter. Ricky's swollen, immobile, and broken hand reached out for mine; his eyes were searching mine, and his cheeks were wet. He wanted me to take his tears. Yet, it wasn't *my* heart that he was giving his tears. It was the heart of Love within me. I was completely overwhelmed by what Love was doing on this infamous street corner on Third that evening.

Not too long afterward, Hollywood was sprawled out on the sidewalk next to the curb, rambling about many things. He called me over; looking into my eyes, he asked me to help him. Hollywood needed his 'brother' (best friend) near him tonight. He didn't want to be alone. I promised Hollywood that I would let his brother know. He gave me his tears as well. I checked in on him throughout the evening as the music of Louie's makeshift street band played on, warming that ignorantly forbidden street corner where Love fought off the wicked talons of hate.

In the midst of all that darkness, light began to penetrate through when Joseph entered the picture at about 11:30 pm. Somehow, he knew our spirits needed a lift. He made us all laugh till our sides ached with his rendition of an old song, modifying the lyrics and hopping around on his one leg, holding the other by the stump singing, *"Does your leg hang low; does it wobble to and fro? Does it swing from side to side?"* Well, you get the picture. Joseph had us all in stitches.

Just after midnight, I asked Joseph if he'd like a shower mentioning I had some salmon steak my daughter gave me. He gladly accepted.

Once we were up in my apartment, Joseph headed into the bathroom. It's easier for Joseph to take a bath rather than a shower. He must have bathed for an hour or more. I fell asleep on my couch and woke up about the same time Joseph finished in the bathroom just in time to witness him enjoy that huge salmon steak. By then, he was completely exhausted.

At times like these, I can't send a person in his situation back out on the streets to search for a doorway or parking garage, where he might get an hour or two of sleep before getting chased off by security or building personnel.

"Joseph, you can stay here tonight," I offered him, pointing across the room to the new twin-size bed I was blessed with after a friendly neighbor passed away in my building just a month before. Brian didn't even have the chance to sleep in his new bed. He died suddenly of heart failure.

Even the bedding and pillows were still in their original packaging when I received them. "You can sleep over there," I said with a smile.

Joseph pointed at the floor next to the bed, "There?" he asked. I guessed he was used to sleeping on the floor.

"No. The bed, silly. I like sleeping on the couch. *You* sleep in the bed."

"Really?" Joseph asked, almost sounding excited.

"Really," I said, reaffirming the offer. The next morning when he awoke, Joseph claimed he hadn't slept that well in a very long time.

I realized that although what I had might be considered simple in our current consumer-focused, convenience-oriented world; where possessions and personal comfort are often more important than helping others—a world where we often lose sight of a home being a place filled with love and support. As a result of opening my heart and home to the outcasts of our society, like Joseph, I now know that the little I have is more than enough. Not just for me but for those who rarely experience an opportunity to sleep inside, where there is acceptance and an absence of judgment. A place of refuge where one can relax and simply be themselves—a home where lonely hearts are loved, just as they are.

To this day, when I hear Joseph singing, his voice echoing throughout the downtown buildings, I am compelled to follow that beautiful sound to find my buddy and enjoy the show!

The Magical Generosity of Zecherieh aka "Zack"

Meeting Zack was truly a Love-send. It was the ledge at that infamous corner on Third that brought us together in 2016. Zack was quiet, 27 years old, five-eleven, having reddish-brown hair cut in a mullet. He is a man of few words unless, of course, he gets riled up. He shared with me that, like so many others on the streets, he is autistic. Zack can get overwhelmed or overstimulated. But what I really want to share about Zack is his thoughtfulness and generosity. In my experience with him, Zack has the heart of a care-taker with an uncanny ability to anticipate one's needs. But most importantly, he truly cares about those he loves and always gives one of the sweetest hugs I've ever experienced.

One evening I invited Jeff and a couple of the other kids to come upstairs for a while. "Can I bring my buddy Zack along?" Jeff asked, promising, "he's good people."

"Sure, come on up," I said, shooting Zack a smile. I was curious about what I might discover in the heart of this seemingly quiet young man.

Once upstairs, everyone settled into a spot. Zack chose to sit in a black pleather chair that swiveled, reclined, and had a separate matching footstool I received from Chris and Gina. Now they were blessing Zack because it became his favorite chair every time he came to visit. And his favorite place to sleep. I believe it was somewhat of a safe place for him when he spent time in my apartment. Zack slept over on other occasions and always in that chair.

Each time Zack came to visit, he always brought cookies or donuts to share, except for the bag of cookies he would stash behind his backpack in the corner of the room by the closet. Once when I had snacks to share, I happened to place them on top of the stove, in the center, telling Zack to help himself. From then on, whenever he had food to share, he placed it in the middle of the stove, even telling his friend Stacy, one afternoon, that it was where the shared snacks belonged. I saw this as Zack's way of respecting my space.

One very remarkable trait of Zack's, which I learned quickly through his visits and overnight stays, is his uncanny ability to anticipate my needs. Without me saying a word, Zack would hand me my keys, shoes, or other items I had forgotten, each time we left my apartment. He would even remind me of my appointments and check in with me about upcoming responsibilities and obligations. He intuitively discerned I was struggling with cognitive challenges and memory problems.

Even more remarkable was the time when we were hanging out, and my feet got cold. I was sitting on my bed barefoot; Zack was in the recliner. Without me having said a word, he silently walked over to my dresser, opened a drawer, and handed me a pair of socks. I just looked at him dumbfounded. "How did you know my feet were cold?" I asked him.

"I dunno," he said. "Just did."

There was an afternoon when one of my best street buddies, Dave, came to hang out. He works hard, so not long after he sat down on the loveseat, having a chance to relax, he fell fast asleep. Zack and two others were visiting as well, but they didn't know Dave, and he did, not yet know them. Anyone who lives on the streets can tell you that it is more common than not that your backpack and belongings may easily get stolen. Dave left his wallet, backpack, and other personal items of value right there in plain sight. Zack not only watched over Dave as he slept, but he made sure all of Dave's belongings stayed right where they were.

On one occasion, I had just bought a used bike. Zack loves skateboards and bicycles. My bike wasn't in the best of condition and was in need of a tune-up and repair. "Can I take it to my camp and work on it for you?" he asked me. His eyes seemed to be filled with light as he looked the bike over. He was very aware that I knew nothing about bicycles. So, when he offered to work on it, and of course, I knew I could trust him, I didn't hesitate.

"Okay, if you want to do that, have at it! And thank you, Zack. I appreciate it. But I don't have any money right now to help with fixing it up."

"Don't worry," he said with an impish grin.

I figured that Zack would tighten up the chain, grease, and lube necessary parts, then probably clean it up. That turned out **not** to be the case at all! About three days later, Zack showed up on Third while I was hanging out with some kids on the corner. He proudly brought a bike over to me. With a smile, he pushed it towards me. I wondered what the heck he was doing? This was a nice bike; it wasn't mine. This one had colorful new fenders, a new seat, and nice hand grips on the handlebars. There was also a bottle holder attached to the inner frame and brand-new lights on both the front and the rear; the handlebars had new brake handles as well.

"What's this? Where's my bike?" I asked, sounding confused.

"This *is* your bike," Zack replied with a smile. "What do you think?"

"*What ...how ...why?*" I stammered in amazement. I started to choke up as I realized Zack had done this for me. A beautiful, unexpected gesture of appreciation and thoughtfulness.

"I just wanted you to have a nice bike," was Zack's humble reply.

"And it is, Zack! Wow, thank you!" I gave him a big hug.

From then on, I noticed Zack silently admiring the bike whenever he saw me riding it. I knew he was proud of his work. I was proud of him too, and grateful for the blessing of Zack's friendship.

One day he helped me out with my chores and even brought me some food. With gratitude, I told Zack I would repay him even though I knew he had no expectations. I began to ponder how I could bless Zack in return. What is it that Zack really loves that I could offer him for repayment? The obvious answer, my bike.

"Hey, Zack. So, what if I give you something in return for all you've done for me today?" I asked matter of factly.

"Like what?" I could tell he was curious and that I had his attention.

"How about that over there in the corner?" I pointed at my bike, leaning against the wall in the corner of my room. Zack turned around to see that I was pointing at my bike.

"Yes!" Zack replied and promised, "I'll take good care of it!"

"I know you will man, that's why I want you to have it. Besides, you really put your heart into fixing it up for me. For many reasons, you really deserve it, Zack."

Zack and the Missing Glasses

In those days, memory issues constantly plagued me, and Zack easily perceived this. I am very nearsighted. I've worn glasses since the age of eleven. I'd take my glasses off in stores, on buses, anywhere I needed to read something up close. It was common for me to set my glasses down somewhere but am unable to see well enough to find them.

I lost the last pair of glasses I owned way before Zack and I met. In fact, he had never seen me wearing glasses. He just knew I'd lost mine and couldn't see well. One day, several months into our friendship, Zack came to my apartment for a visit. We sat at the table in front of the large picture window. He pulled something out of his backpack and handed it to me. It was a pair of glasses.

"Here, try these on. See if they work," Zack offered me.

"Glasses? Oh, it's rare that any prescription will match mine. I have astigmatism." I said to him, almost handing them back.

"No, go ahead and try them," he insisted.

"Okay. I'll give them a try," I said, having already convinced myself that there was no use in trying them on. As I unfolded the pair, I noticed that the frame looked familiar. "Hmmm," I thought. "That's odd," I put them on. They rested perfectly balanced on my face. But that wasn't the best part. The best part was that I could see *PERFECTLY!* These were an identical prescription to the glasses I'd lost months before. I grabbed them off my face and took another look. These eyeglasses were far more than just familiar; I recognized a small scratch on the frame. These **were** the glasses I had lost months before!

"Zack! Dude!" I cried out. "Where the heck did you find these?! Look at this scratch here," I said, pointing at the frame. "I can see perfectly with them! These aren't just the same prescription as mine; these *are my glasses!* I lost these a few months back!"

"I found them under a tree in Waterfront Park," Zack explained.

"What the heck! Are you some kind of angel? This is amazing!" I gushed, in awe of what I saw as a miracle. Zack merely looked glad that he was able to help.

Now and again, Zack spent the night or brought his girlfriend, Mariah, or a buddy to visit. But anytime I am on Third, in Waterfront Park, or under the Burnside Bridge, and Zack spots me, he comes zipping up on his bike, knowing I will open my arms wide and give him a big bear hug. And truly, this old guy never wants to let go.

Zecherieh ~ "Good times, Zack ... I'll always love you man and look forward to hanging out with ya! You're a blessing AND pure love, dude!"

~Poppa Chuck

Mariah Jean aka "Max"

When I first met Max, my buddy Zack introduced us at the ledge in the fall of 2016. He proudly stated, "This is my girlfriend, Mariah." Honored that Zack chose to introduce his girlfriend to me, I was soon to find that she was a feisty, yet, very sweet and sensitive young lady.

Max and Zack spent that first evening after our introduction chatting away in my apartment, the two of them bantering back and forth. They were funny as heck!

We shared food, laughter, and (for this old guy) the joy of each other's company. That evening was the beginning of a tender bond between Max and me, a friendship that paused for a little over a year until we randomly met again at a day center in NE Portland. (I begin to wonder, is it ever 'random' or 'coincidence' when people reunite?)

Max spotted me first at that day center, where she was having breakfast as a guest of a dear friend of hers. I struggled a bit with knowing from where I knew this young woman, but soon it all came back, and warm hugs filled the atmosphere of a dreary church basement that morning.

Again, just a few weeks later, Max and I found ourselves standing in line together at Pioneer Courthouse Square, waiting in the sunshine for free donuts, coffee, and bus tickets. This was another loving reunion where we realized that staying connected was important to each of us. We chose social network as our best avenue and were soon connecting nearly every day, with Max beginning to reveal her life's daily challenges and struggles.

At just 20 years of age, Max strains to connect to life as she deals with numerous physical and mental health issues. She shared her story with me over a cup of hot chocolate at a Starbucks on a cold December day in 2018. With compassion and understanding welling up within me, I learned the bitter depth of Max's mostly heartbreaking story over the sweet taste of hot chocolate and whipped cream.

Max had been in and out of foster care for most of her life. Only a year before we met, she aged out of the system. After that, she spent two months in a hotel. Her biological mother came and got her at that point, which sadly turned out to be an unhealthy situation for Max, where her mother's own struggles hindered the blossoming of a long-lost relationship. Since then, Max has had a tough time getting off the streets and into housing, where she hopes to be safe and happy one day.

"When I first became homeless, I was in Tillamook, Oregon. I was completely alone and lost at the time. I didn't know what to do or where to go. I was really scared. I made it to a church, Tillamook Christian Center. It's the church where I first accepted Jesus. When they sang a song called 'Where Feet May Fail,' I completely lost it and bawled my eyes out for an hour. This song has saved me more than once since then," Max shared with me.

"Oceans (Where Feet May Fail)"

By Hillsong UNITED

https://www.youtube.com/watch?v=dy9nwe9_xzw

Max briefly mentioned one of her parents during our hot chocolate chat. She felt it to be an important part of her story. "[My parent] was verbally, emotionally, and physically abusive to me. There is only one thing [they] taught me. That I'll never amount to anything! When I was a little girl, I told [them] I wanted to be a veterinarian when I grew up. I really wanted to become a vet, and I thought sharing would make [them] proud of me. Instead, I was told, 'You will *never* do that!'"

Max says she has since moved past the abuse but not the trauma. She works each day NOT to allow those hateful words to maintain a grip on her thoughts or have power over her any longer. "But I don't go see my family because of that," she told me. "I want to someday, but for now, I just can't."

"I love music, and I love singing. The song 'Another Empty Bottle' means a lot to me because of everything I went through while growing up." This old guy completely relates to Max's story and this song. I'd not heard it before, but I am grateful that Max shared it with me, for it speaks to the tragedy and resulting trauma of a broken home due to the destructive power of alcoholism. Please take the time to check out the song and video.

"Another Empty Bottle"

By Katy Mcallister

https://www.youtube.com/watch?v=jcuaA-nJF_0

Max admits that she often pushes people away and has zero self-esteem. But even worse, she has a very difficult time having compassion for herself, although she has a great deal of compassion for others. This brought her to thinking about Zack. "I still love Zack, but I realize we're not meant to be together."

During our chat, we touched on her personal experience with homelessness. "The hardest part of being homeless is wondering where the next meal might come from. There are times when I need to use a restroom. People working at local businesses yell at me, *'NO!! YOU JUST WANT TO DO DRUGS IN THE RESTROOM... GET OUT OF HERE!'*" "I don't do drugs. Just the medicinal marijuana to help with my anxiety and PTSD," she explained to me.

This young lady is a talented vocalist. "I started singing when I was only five years old. I like songs that mean something to me. 'I Can Only Imagine' by MercyMe, and there are so many songs by Jesus Culture that I really like. When I sang at home growing up, it would quiet the arguments going on between my parents." Sadly, conflicts and arguments were more common in Max's home than not.

"Singing to my little sister, Arya, would always calm her during the arguments between my parents. She means the world to me. She is AMAZING! Our song was "Orinoco Flow" by Enya. The lyrics comforted both of us when nothing else would."

Max's dream is to open a daycare someday for autistic kids and those with Down Syndrome. She has a huge heart for these members of our society. This old guy appreciates Max's heart after having joyfully worked alongside these individuals myself over the years; a HIGH-POINT of my life story. It makes me even more proud of my sassy and sweet streetheart, Max.

Out of the Belly of the Lite Rail:
My own personal "Jonah and the Whale Tale"
(MY plans are NOT always Love's plans)

There are times when I unexpectedly find myself called into the midst of the struggles that prevail over the lives of the untraditionally housed population here in Portland. A mom may message me from somewhere on the East Coast wondering if I have seen her son, or a social network post by one of the kids might prompt me to take a walk to check in with some of my street buddies. Or an extremely cold night itself might call me out to see what needs there may be on the streets. One time, even my good buddy David came to take me to a young street woman who was suffering from the trauma of physical and sexual abuse.

One of those times was when the concerns of a caring mother in Massachusetts, worried about her son, took me to the downtown area on a cold Saturday evening in December of 2018. It had been a long day, a long week for that matter, in the life of this busy old guy. I was extremely exhausted, needed rest, and still had things to do. But checking on Gutter (you will meet him in Chapter Six) was certainly a priority at that moment and something I'd already planned to do even before I heard from his mom.

My walk around the SW downtown business district failed to locate Gutter or other kids. I felt increasingly exhausted, and I knew I needed to head home and rest. That's when my phone notified me that Max had sent me a message.

"Hey," was her simple message before she added, "Can I come by for a few?"

I wasn't sure how to respond. She'd never asked me if she could come to my place before. I was so exhausted at that moment, thinking to myself, "I'd better start taking care of myself, or I might start getting rundown and sick. I messaged her back, "I'm not home. What's up?"

"Oh, just kinda need a friend."

"I'm sorry I'm not there. I'll be around tomorrow," I wrote, thinking I'd be more rested and readily available.

Max's simple reply, "Ok."

I was NOT comfortable with this messenger chat at all! Max had been living in a youth shelter just a block from my apartment for a couple of months. She'd been struggling with relationship issues, her self-worth, depression, and suicidal thoughts, as well as hurting herself. I wished I weren't so rundown. I could only hope that Gutter, Mama Kat, and Max would all be fine.

I headed to the MAX Station for a ride back home and jumped onto a random car. Usually, I ride in the back car of the lite rail since I live right next to the station at Providence Park. Then, when I exit from the rear car,

I'm practically at my front door. But whether it was exhaustion, or me just not paying attention, *OR* some *cosmic reason*, I mindlessly stepped onto a car closer to the front of the train.

It was just 10 days before Christmas; weary holiday shoppers packed the lite rails that evening. It was standing room only and seemed much too long of a trip for me. I just needed to be at home.

"Providence Park, doors to my right," I was relieved to hear the overhead speakers announce as the train began slowing down into the station. *Then*, as the car came to a stop, the door windows brought two individuals into view even though it was dark outside. There were sounds of anger and shouting; not something particularly unusual for this area. Fearful that my PTSD might kick in, I instinctively wondered, *"What the heck is going on out there?!"*

The doors immediately slid open, and there, standing right in front of me as I stepped off the train, was Max, shouting at a TriMet Security Officer. She was obviously in distress. As the other patrons attempted to steer away from the shouting and the intensity of the situation, I slowly walked into it.

"Max, sweetheart," I said gently. "Are you okay?" I kept my eyes focused on her, realizing the security guard was next to me on my left, standing between Max, the train, and the tracks. I stayed focused on making sure Max was okay.

"NO! Poppa Chuck!" Max shouted, holding her hand up as if to keep me away. "I thought you weren't home! He can't make me go! *I won't go! He needs to leave me alone!*"

I stood still, giving Max a gentle nod, "I'm just getting home. I'll give you some space if you'd like."

"Make him leave me alone!" Max shouted. Then she stormed away in the opposite direction, continuing to yell as she looked back over her shoulder.

I turned to the TriMet Security Guard, "I know this young woman. I will stay with her to make sure she is okay." He nodded at me while I began walking in Max's direction. She was already crossing a street as patrol cars pulled up, stopping next to her. The officers got out of their vehicles, and

Max began shouting at them, *"YOU CAN'T MAKE ME GO! I WON'T GO TO THE HOSPITAL AGAIN! YOU CAN'T MAKE ME!"*

There were three officers: one female and two males. "We just want to talk to you for a minute," one of the officers explained to her.

"NO!" Max shouted back as she continued down 17th Street towards Burnside. *"I WON'T GO TO THE HOSPITAL! YOU'RE NOT GO-ING TO MAKE ME!"* With that, Max disappeared behind a building. I was now next to the officers. I could see compassion on their faces. I began to understand that this was not a new situation for Max.

"Officers, I know this young woman. She feels safe with me. I will make sure she is okay."

"Who are you?" one of the officers asked.

"I'm just a friend. I look after some of the street youth. I love them and make sure they know someone cares about them. Is it okay if you let me handle this one?"

"Well, technically," the officer stated, "We have to take her in." I sensed or maybe wanted to believe that the officer said 'technically' be-cause they were hopeful that I could help Max. They did their duty, but they also opened the door for another heart to enter the picture and walk alongside a very distraught young woman.

"What happened?" I asked.

"She tried to jump in front of that train," he informed me as we both looked in the direction of the train I'd just ridden. It was now pulling away from the station.

I didn't have time to process what he'd just told me. "I've walked through these episodes with her before. She'll be ok. Just give me some time with her. Please!" I implored the officers.

"What is her name?" he asked.

"Max," I offered him.

"Do you know her last name?"

"No," I said, but, in truth, had I taken the time, I could've looked her up on social network to give it to them, but I was more fearful for Max at that moment, wanting to find her and be at her side.

"You think you can help her, go on," he said. "Let us know if you need our help."

"Okay, thank you," I said with a forced smile. "She'll be okay, I promise."

With that said, I walked down the street in the direction Max had gone. Once I reached Alder Street and Burnside, I realized she was no-where in sight. 'DANG!' I thought to myself. 'Where the heck did she go?'

I wondered if she might have gone to McDonald's just two blocks away. So, I headed in that direction, keeping my eyes peeled. Within five minutes, I was inside McDonald's on West Burnside, and still no sign of her.

'An ice cream,' I thought to myself. 'I'm going to sit here and eat an ice cream and try to reach her on social network. Maybe I can get her to come and join me.'

I quickly purchased a vanilla soft serve ice cream cone (one of my favorite comfort foods), keeping one eye on the entrance in case she might walk in and the other eye on my phone. I wanted to make sure I didn't miss her. With ice cream in hand, I chose to sit at a table that gave me a view of the entrance. Then, just as I pulled my phone out of my pocket, to my relief, a message popped up from Max.

Even though I love vanilla soft serve ice cream and in my own state of distress over being exhausted, I *really needed* that ice cream, respond-ing to Max was far more important. I placed a napkin down on the table, then carefully stood my cone upright on the napkin so I could message her back.

"I'm sorry 😔," Max wrote to me.

"Why? You're fine. We're fine. I convinced the officers to let me help you. They're gone now."

"Thanks. I'm down the road."

"You know I love you."

"I love you too. I'm sorry. I hate myself."

"I just thought you might need some space. I'm holding out for the miracle."

"I want to see you. I'm straight down the hill on the other side of Burnside, sitting in a doorway."

"I'm at McDonald's. Want an ice cream?"

"Yes, I'll be right there."

Moments later, Max walked through the door. I left my ice cream, standing it up again on the table to greet her and give her a big, long fatherly hug.

"I'm sorry," she told me. "I've been in a really bad situation and didn't know how to handle it. I'm so tired of men taking advantage of me."

"You're fine," I said. "Come, let's get you an ice cream, then we'll talk. What kind would you like?"

"Vanilla. I'll take vanilla," came her sheepish reply.

I offered her a soda as well but added, "Wait! Have you eaten today?"

"No," came another sheepish reply.

"Let's get you a burger and fries then."

"Really? That would really help," Max said, sounding a little better.

Once we were seated at the table (my ice cream cone still standing upright), she began telling me, while scarfing down her burger, how she was targeted by sex traffickers on social network. I was sickened by this information. "I blocked and reported them, though," she assured me. We chatted about meeting men online and the dangers. Max told me a guy friend of hers was on his way to meet her there at McDonald's. He was going to stay with her so she'd not be alone and would be safe. She wanted me to stay until he arrived and hoped I could meet him.

"I'd like that," I told her, then promised, "I won't leave you alone." It was then that I gently asked her, "But Max, is what the officers said ... was it true? Did you try to jump in front of the train?"

"Yes," she admitted. "I just wanted to die."

I hung my head in silence for a moment, then asked, "You feeling better now?"

"Yes. I guess I needed to eat. Thank you," she smiled her first smile since this whole ordeal had started. It meant a great deal to me. We then chatted about the youth shelter she was staying in and a recent failed relationship as we waited for her friend. I listened as Max shared with me her current fears and anguish. There was no need to judge or offer advice. Max simply needed someone who cared, and was there for her. I was so blessed and am forever grateful that it got to be me.

Three months later, I received this text message from Max ..."Hey, do you know what I was just thinking about? I was thinking about that night when I was going to jump in front of the MAX [train]. When you got off the train, I was so scared that I had let you down."

"But you didn't. 🖤"

"I hope not."

"NO! Don't even think that. I was so grateful I could be there. It was a 'God shot!'"

"I love you so much!"

"I love YOU TOO, MAX! You're AMAZING! Sleep well. 🖤"

"Thank you. I'll message you tomorrow."

This post Max put on the social network in the winter of 2019. I'm not a worrier, but this old guy's heart ached for my sweet friend as the months went by after she posted this, with not a word from Max. I feared (even grieving) that I would need to move her story to the last chapter of the book, "Sidewalks to Heaven."

A chapter about those we've lost from the streets. But to my relief and delight, Max resurfaced through a text message. She was safe with her family in Newport, Oregon. It was but a few weeks later that Max returned to Portland.

Fast forward a year; Max now communicates with me wherever she is. She travelled across the country to relocate, eventually entering a transitional housing program in Pennsylvania.

One day, to my surprise, Max checked in with me, telling me about her fiancé. They want to have a child someday. Max said she had told her fiancé all about me and the book. A message from Max in the summer of 2020 revealed that she and her beau (when they would become parents sometime in the future), wanted me to be the godfather of their child. Humbled, I wholeheartedly said, "Yes."

Once Max returned to Portland, she and I got together at a Starbuck's. I wanted to surprise her with the opportunity to look through a paper copy of the manuscript. Up until then, she had only heard about the book. She'd never actually seen a paper copy. As Max quietly looked in awe through the pages, she said, "It's *really* happening!"

"Yes, sweetheart, with your participation, undying encouragement, and help, it's *REALLY* happening!

~ Poppa Chuck

"A father's blessing, I speak over my precious street-daughter, Mariah "Max" Jean: May you experience the joy of living 'life to the FULL,' and may your joy be complete as you walk in the light of Love. May your hope always be in the love that encompasses all of humanity. May your heart ALWAYS be filled with love and compassion, not only for others but, most importantly, for yourself. ALWAYS KNOW, without a doubt, this old guy loves you dearly."

~Poppa Chuck

I suppose meeting these beautiful street characters thus far would be enough to open my heart to loving the outcasts of our world unconditionally. But Love's plan was to take me much deeper than that as I entered a journey into my own heart as well as through meeting a whole community of endearing characters (the untraditionally housed) called the Dirty Kids.

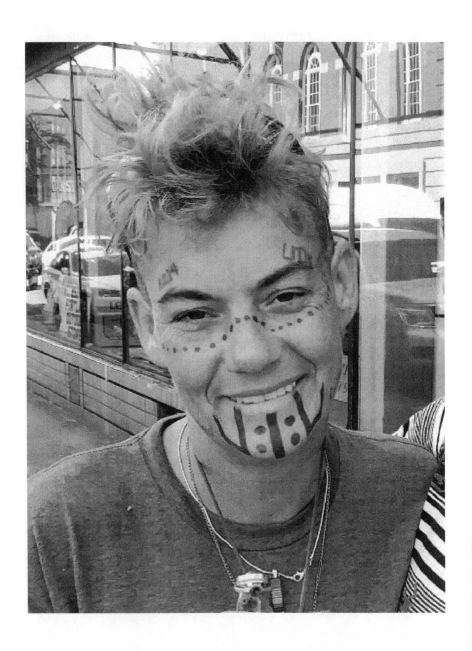

Chapter Five

"Sidewalk" Sarah & The Dirty Kids

"Sidewalk"

A street community and Dirty Kid legend in downtown Portland AND across the U.S.

"To me, my whole life has been pretty normal, parents are divorced, met a guy, had some kids, a house. Then that started to fall apart. I developed chronic migraines. We split up; I moved on to a new state. Then outta nowhere, I met a Dirty Kid, learned a whole new lifestyle, made a bunch of new friends, and got away with more shit [than] imaginable."

"When I talk about myself, I always say, 'Sidewalk.' It's hard to be Sarah. Sarah is shy and quiet. I haven't been that in a long time. Sidewalk is always there. I find my strength in Sidewalk. She's done more than Sarah ever could." ~*Sidewalk*

When Sidewalks Smile isn't about Sidewalk herself, but she is one of the many beautiful sidewalks these stories tell of. Back in the day, Sidewalk was always there on SW Third Street, unless invited inside somewhere, or off traveling the country or visiting family.

She is one of downtown's landmarks. In essence, Sidewalk warms the hearts of many of us with her hugs, and she always knows when I need one. Most often, Sidewalk sports outlandish colorful hairstyles and appropriate Dirty Kid street attire.

The Dirty Kids are a subculture of home-free nomads who travel the country by hopping trains. They live a very simple lifestyle, essentially off-grid. The train hoppers call themselves Travelers, while the Dirty Kids who prefer to settle in one place yet maintain that 'home-free' lifestyle call themselves, Homebums. They see the world far differently than society sees it—something I find to be very refreshing and intriguing.

The Dirty Kids I've come to know and love are beautiful souls, and many are very talented musicians with a focus on the American Folk music genre. I did not learn until later, but Louie is a Dirty Kid. Busking (performing on street corners for money) is one way they earn money but more importantly, most of the Dirty Kids I've met long for change in our world where compassion and unconditional love encompasses all. They share their joys, sorrows, and enlightening perspectives on life with anyone who will take the time to listen. Some of them spange (asking for spare change) as they hang out sewing their own clothes, cutting each other's hair, writing songs, poems, and even giving each other tattoos on the sidewalks of our cities. Some have clever jokes they tell for a buck, which often turns into meaningful conversations about life and the need for a kinder and more caring world.

Sidewalk graces our sidewalks, at the curb's edge, living a simple life and caring for her friends. She is most often welcoming the passers-by with her loud and seemingly cantankerous greetings. And, yes, Sidewalk gets grumpy at times, like any one of us. But such is life, especially living on the streets where your living room, dining room, and bedroom are a glasshouse, where your everyday life is out there for everyone to see.

I met Sidewalk shortly after I met Jeff. At first, I wondered if she was one of those aggressive panhandlers when she asked me for spare change the first time. I simply told her I was penniless but would help if I could.

"No worries," she said with a smile.

"But I can give you a hug," I offered her. She stood without hesitating. I'll never forget that first Dirty Kid hug, so warm like she truly cared about me. After that, I always got a hug from Sidewalk every time I walked by. Soon I was stopping to chat frequently and eventually warming that sidewalk, along with her and her friends, for brief periods during the day. For me, there was always so much love.

There were evenings when sitting out on Third with Sidewalk and her friends was a welcome respite from being inside. I learned something new from those visits with Sidewalk and her friends; I learned that the nightlife traffic is very busy in that part of downtown. And although Sidewalk beckoned people to visit by attempting to get a laugh, most people walked on by.

One of the ways she attempted to get a laugh out of almost anyone in the vicinity was to shout out, *"You want to see my tiny penis?"* Some would stop, but most would sail on past her as if she weren't there.

At first, I was silently horrified when I heard her ask a group of older adults if they wanted to see her tiny penis. But then she turned to me with an impish giggle. She held out her necklace, asking, *"You want to see my tiny penis, Chuck?"* I was extremely reluctant to look, but for the sake of Sidewalk, I glanced down to see her holding a tiny brass charm between her thumb and index finger; *YES*, it *is* a tiny penis. I laughed out loud when I realized it was a gag. I found it to be a hilarious test, if you will, to see whether people will judge before they learn the truth.

During these brief visits in the evenings on Third with Sidewalk and the gang, I learned that most people ignore the Dirty Kids. I realize that I have done the same all of my life, even avoiding a whole city block to steer away from the 'undesirables.' Now, sitting there on the pavement with Sidewalk and friends, this new perspective was challenging everything I had ignorantly thought about street people. These guys are pretty cool and fun-loving.

The well-dressed college-age adults, obviously privileged, mocked and rebuked the unseemly pavement dwellers with an attitude of superiority. *"GET A JOB! GET A LIFE, YOU LOWLIFES!"* Scorn was a daily ritual performed by several in the community, inflicting it upon the outcasts of our society. I never imagined it was this bad. I also learned that intoxication played a key role in the contemptuous behavior of the privileged as well. I wondered if they were even aware of their condescending and judgmental behavior. It even took on the appearance of being a 'sport' to them; laughing and mocking the meek and lowly was fair game.

The Dirty Kids were used to this treatment. So much so they didn't bat an eye and rarely even commented on it. The common response to being ignored was one of the kids respectfully saying, "Have a nice day." I marvel at this every time I hear a street person say it because, certainly, that would *not* be my response. I realized that I have much to learn about grace from the Dirty Kids.

On those evening visits, the beauty, for me, was the folks (young and old) that stopped to chat like they were old friends. Many offered food, drinks, or cash, and sometimes even Voodoo Donuts. There was laughter and lighthearted conversation. It was always a delight to witness the love people shared with the street community. Oftentimes it was simply good conversation with those who stopped to offer a listening ear that manifested love on the sidewalks.

One Friday afternoon, I was preparing to leave town to visit family for the Mother's Day weekend and needed to get a couple of things at the store. On my walk to the store, I saw Sidewalk walking towards me. At that moment, I remembered her telling me about her kids who live in Indiana with her mom. I wondered how long it had been since she'd seen them. I also wondered if Sidewalk knew that Sunday was Mother's Day and how that might affect her.

"Hey Chuck," came Sidewalk's familiar voice as we walked up to one another. Sidewalk gave me a huge hug as always.

After the hug, I held onto Sidewalk's shoulders, "I need to mention something that might be hard to hear."

Sidewalk looked down at the ground, "Oh no, you're going to tell me something bad has happened."

"No, Sidewalk," I assured her. "It's something good but might be hard for you to hear at first. Look up at me." I used one finger to gently lift her chin upwards till her eyes met mine. Softly I said, "Did you know Sunday is Mother's Day?"

"Oh, BALLS!" she said with a bit of relief. "I thought you were going to tell me someone died!"

"No," I smiled at her. "I just know that you miss your kids, and I wanted to wish you a happy Mother's Day before I left town for the weekend."

Sidewalk looked a little sad. "Yeah, I miss them," she said somberly. "Thank you for telling me. My son is a Marine!" she added, attempting to sound strong.

"You must be very proud of him," I offered her.

"I am," she stated, again looking down at the pavement.

"Look, I gotta get ready to leave town. I love you, sweetheart." I then asked, "Are you gonna be okay?"

"Yeah," Sidewalk replied. "It's all good." But she still seemed to be in a somber mood. I hated to leave her at that moment, but I needed to get ready and be at the bus station on time. I made it to the store, purchased the items, and headed back to my apartment.

Once I got my things packed, I put my backpack on and headed down the street in the opposite direction of Sidewalk's 'spot' on Third. I was still hoping she was okay. Then something really special happened. I heard Sidewalk hollering from down Third Street. But this time she sounded really happy.

"Chuck!" her voice called out to me from across the street, nearly a block away. Over the sound of the traffic, she hollered, *"Have a good weekend, Chuck! I love you! I'll see you when you get back!"*

Sidewalk waved at me using her whole body and every ounce of her being. I not only heard her words of love, but I *felt* them deeply resonating within me, which I swear lasted that entire bus ride to my hometown. That was when I realized Sidewalk was family. I was leaving one precious family here in Portland to visit another. There was now more love in my life than ever.

One day I came across a pretty summer dress a friend was giving away. I immediately thought of Sidewalk even though I'd only seen her in leather, chain mail, fatigues, and canvas coveralls. This dress was white with large fluorescent green flowers. I knew immediately it was meant for Sidewalk. When I brought it to her, she was elated!

"Cool!" Sidewalk screamed. *"Stay right here with my stuff. I'll be right back!"* It was only moments later when she reappeared wearing that dress. It fit her perfectly and made that sidewalk we stood upon even more beautiful than ever. I hadn't seen my friend in a dress before. This was a real treat for both of us.

"So, Sidewalk," I was afraid to ask. "Where did you change into the dress?" Sidewalk pointed to the parking lot behind me, all the while looking down, admiring her new dress, and twirling around like a young schoolgirl.

"I changed behind those cars," She explained nonchalantly, still twirling about. "*AND,* I peed."

Such is the world of our Sidewalk. I laugh out loud as I write this; the endearing and precocious world of *The Sidewalk.*

When Sidewalk leaves town, Third Street becomes completely devoid of Dirty Kids. It is lonely walking in that area of town when she is not around. Yet, Sidewalk calls me while traveling across the country on her adventures. Traveling from Illinois to Arkansas on one occasion, she just *had* to tell me about her new dog, Buddy. Most often, she calls to say, "Hey," or, "I love you," and always adds, "I'll check in with you soon!" Moments like this, hearing Sidewalk so happy, they mean the world to me.

On many of her road trips, Sidewalk visits with people that she considers her family, like Kellee Brookheart. She shared this with me one afternoon: *"I Love Sarah with all of my heart. She raised me and was the best mother figure a girl could ask for. She coached softball, hosted sleepovers, took us on nature walks, taught us how to cook, how to clean, gave us 'the talk,' taught us the beauty of the outdoors, let us dress how we wanted, do our hair how we wanted, taught us how to have fun* [and make the best of] *of any situation, and most importantly she taught us not to care what other people said or thought of us. She is, and always will be, a huge part of my heart. My children love her too. She comes every winter to visit, and they ask at least once a week when she will be back. She is so very special."*

The day I was encouraged to write this book by friends who were following my street adventures on a social network, I got excited and even more inspired. I began to ponder the adventures, where they began, and with whom? *"The sidewalks!"* I declared out loud while alone in my apartment. "Sidewalk's Smile" and "When Sidewalks Smile" (using Sidewalk's name as a pun) both were fun titles for a book. Now I wanted Sidewalk and Freddy to know how their love for me, and our friendship, had inspired me to write the stories about them and their friends.

The first chance I got, I walked to Sidewalk's spot on Third (well, maybe ran). She sat, as usual, next to the curb, sewing a patch on a garment while Freddy sat next to her, sanding a skateboard. *"Sidewalk, Freddy!"* I whispered emphatically. "I gotta tell you something exciting. I've been writing stories about my adventures out here with you guys and the other kids and posting them on a social network. My friends all love the stories and want me to turn them into a book. I'm going to call it Sidewalk's Smile or When Sidewalks Smile! I want the world to see you guys like I do, all the beauty and the love that you guys are to me! What do you think?" The response was beautiful. Sidewalk, Freddy, and the rest encouraged me, offering to tell more of their stories.

In the spring of 2019, I ran into Sidewalk, Buddy, Gutter, Jason, and Elan. "We're really hungry, Chuck! Can I come to your place and cook us some food? Please, please, please?" Sidewalk begged me.

It didn't take much for me to cave unless I had obligations. "Are you wanting to get Papa Murphy's Take and Bake?" I offered, hoping the cooking session would be short and sweet.

"No …Gutter can't eat that!" she reminded me.

'Ah, yes, wheat,' I thought to myself. Gutter is such a sensitive guy in so many ways.

"I want to go to Safeway or Fred Meyer to get a few things and cook a real dinner. I have food stamps," she said, explaining her plan to me.

"Okay, but what are you doing with Buddy? No dogs allowed." I reminded her.

"He's a Service Dog; they have to let him in," she informed me.

"It's not just the building management's rules; it's my rule as well. No dogs. Even though I love Buddy and would enjoy taking him along with us, he needs to stay outside. Can someone watch him?"

"Okay," Sidewalk caved, with a fleeting tone of disappointment in her voice. "Gutter, will you stay with Buddy? We'll be back with dinner." Gutter agreed, saying he would wait. Sidewalk and I left the others near the ledge on Third. Hopefully, we would return within a couple of hours.

A stop at the Stadium Fred Meyer on West Burnside was another eye-opening experience for this old guy. *Everyone* working in that huge store knew Sidewalk by name. Most of them call her Sarah. I wondered at the time why that was but stopped myself. Maybe I didn't want to know.

"Chuck. I want you to see if you can find a few things for me. I'll meet you at the cash register." She sounded almost cryptic.

86

"Okay. I'll see you there in a couple of minutes." Something told me Sidewalk was sparing me from something, or maybe I just imagined it.

Five minutes later, we met at the Self-Checkout registers. She quickly scanned all the items, paid with her EBT card, and said, "C'mon, we gotta go."

We had walked only a few feet when I heard two employees calling out, "Sarah, wait, you dropped something." I looked back to see a package of Tampons lying on the floor next to our register.

"It's not mine," she said quickly, rushing me out the door. There, she explained to me that she didn't have money to purchase feminine products. Something told me that the store would have likely given her the products if she'd asked. But Sidewalk is often in survival mode. I was beginning to understand more about her life by walking her path alongside her.

We were at my building and up in my apartment before we knew it. Sidewalk updated me on her life while she prepared the food in the kitchen. She had purchased center-cut pork loins, fresh potatoes, and carrots, along with a few other things. She can talk a mile a minute, and I wondered if she was paying attention to what she was doing while she chatted. I updated her on the book while stressing about the food turning out well.

A special part of our time together was me noticing a familiar 'dance' I've seen my buddy Doug do hundreds of times while he is preparing a meal. He loves to cook and does it extremely well. He can make a wonderful meal, not only tasty but the aromas are heavenly. Sidewalk reminded me so much of Doug at this moment. She was definitely in her element.

"You like to cook, don't you?" I asked.

"Yup," she replied. "I was accepted into Bobby Flay's Cooking School years ago. I think my dad kept the letter."

"What happened? Is it still something you want to do?" I asked her.

"I got pregnant. And my life is different now. But I love to cook any chance I get." She glanced up at me and reassured me with a smile.

"WOW, Sidewalk! I discover more wonderful things about you all the time. This is good stuff!"

Then she went back to talking a mile a minute. She wanted me to know about how Marilyn Manson's music had helped get her through several difficult years as a teen. They were dark times for Sarah. She said that it seemed Manson's songs spoke to her, making things easier.

Later, I took the time to listen to a few of those songs. They were dark and horrific. But I knew that if Sidewalk was comforted by them, then who was I to judge? "Everything serves a purpose," is what Sidewalk and I would hear our dear friend Joe Paulicivic say in moments like these. They were comforting words for certain.

Before I knew it, Sidewalk declared dinner was ready, directing me to help pack it up. I sampled each entree, finding it all to be delicious! Then we were off on the Max and back at the ledge where Buddy, Gutter, and Josh still sat waiting for us. Sidewalk effortlessly laid all the food out on the ledge while the guys patiently waited.

When she said, "Come and get it." They pounced on the food, devouring it, and moaning in ecstasy at how wonderful it was to have a real home-cooked meal. All prepared by the capable hands of our Sidewalk. A true blessing that girl is to so many.

The day I handed her the release form for the When Sidewalks Smile Project, giving permission to publish photos, stories, etc., Sidewalk was elated! Then she did something unexpected. As she and Freddy sat on the sidewalk in front of my apartment building with all their gear and Buddy sprawled out on the pavement trying to stay cool, she grabbed a backpack. Scavenging through it, Sidewalk pulled out a blue soft-cover book with a clasp on it. Shoving it at me, she said. "Here, keep this for a while. It will help with my story." It was her journal. I was shocked, honored, and overjoyed that she would trust me to keep it safe and read through it without question. I felt like I'd been given a treasure chest of precious jewels to openly share with the world.

The following is my favorite entry from her journal. A profound message of divine purpose:

"The gods came to me the other day. In one of my rants to them. They told me I am not allowed to come home until I can make everyone care. Not just about stuff and things but life itself. Other people's lives. The world needs to reconnect with itself. We are all one. If we can't learn to care and protect each other, we're [screwed]!

I screamed and cried, 'That is too much to ask of me! How could I ever?'

They replied, '[Because] YOU... are the SIDEWALK!'"

Something that has been tearing me up inside is the turmoil and (sometimes perceived) chaos that seems to surround our notorious Sidewalk, as well as her beloved friends. Arrests for 'trespassing' (camping in unwelcome downtown areas), court appearances, and visits from police officers are commonplace. And then there are Sidewalk's rants (sometimes misunderstood and misjudged) on the sidewalks of Third Street. At times, all of this has made me wonder (albeit briefly) if I'm way off track with writing about many of these individuals. It leaves me wondering if the heart of this project is a bit askew. But Love brings me back to my senses as I write, edit, and reread these stories. Every one of these true stories, from this old guy's perspective, is beautiful and loving.

One evening when I was home in an extremely hot unairconditioned apartment, having been pulled in countless different directions all day with very little self-care and text messages from four different people looking for a safe place to stay for the night. I needed some me time and was stressing myself out by having to reply to these requests with, "Not tonight. It's not a good night." I had often allowed guilt to sabotage my mental health.

Because of the extreme heat in my apartment, I had my door to the nicely air-conditioned hallway propped open and an oscillating fan placed in the doorway, welcoming the cool air into my room.

I stood in the kitchen in front of the fan, stressing and trying to cool and calm myself, when unexpectedly, my door swung open, pushing the fan aside. Sidewalk was entering the already anxiety-riddled atmosphere that was actually taking place within me.

To my surprise, in a self-preservation mode, and in what I see now as my own 'Sidewalk-like' reaction, I said, "No Sidewalk, this isn't okay. I need you to use the callbox downstairs to enter the building. I need you to go out now; it's not a good time!"

I chased her off because of the overwhelming dilemma I was in. I felt really bad, especially since she left in tears. The thing is, this was traumatic for both of us. Yet, it helped me to see more clearly from the inside look-ing out, a glimpse into Sidewalk's world and her own stressors. Now I understand what she experiences on the streets and sidewalks when others are entering her space, and she is dealing with her own anxiety, migraines, exhaustion, hunger, and feelings of being pulled in too many directions at once. And the truth was, Sidewalk *had* used the callbox. She was taking food to a disabled man she knew, living just down the hall from me.

When this truth began to unfold in my mind and become very clear to me, my heart softened for my dear friend in countless ways. I was now blessed with a window into Sidewalk's struggles, knowing she can deal with chronic migraines and the challenges that come with living on the streets. But, the most beautiful part of this experience was that it is vital to this project to share a glimpse into the trauma often experienced by the untraditionally housed.

With all the difficult things our street community deals with daily; the sweeps by police, evictions from their camps [their homes], trespassing charges (sleeping in the wrong place at the wrong time); these truths help this old guy to write about the tough stuff going on with Sidewalk. There are relationship problems, arrests, questionable behavior (accusations of lighting sidewalks on fire), and yelling at people on the streets. I think I get it now. I lose it at times as well. Boy, do I!

I hope that by sharing these experiences, it helps one to see into the unseen world of Sidewalk's daily stressors. This is not an attempt at ex-plaining things away, making excuses, or victimizing our girl. It simply is a window into the world of the sidewalks and the amazing truth that some-how, through all the trauma and drama, with tragedies and heartbreak around nearly every corner, there is still love. Let us revel in the beauty of the precious moments where love shouts out through all of it and *where sidewalks resiliently smile.*

For far too long, I had worried about not having anything to offer in sharing about the heart of our endearing Sidewalk. I even stressed about it. Yet Love had a plan all along. The stories were treasures buried deep in my heart. I just needed to be patient and let Love guide me in accessing the memories.

The day I got a message on social network from Sidewalk's mother, Wendy, I was elated! What an unexpected gift! I offered to send her the segment about her daughter via email. After reading it, she wrote me back:

> "I'm in tears! This is so beautifully written. Cutting this short, hard to type thru tears. But that's my beautiful daughter. When young, she and a friend collected can goods for a project at school to feed the poor. They wrote their names on each and every can or box of food. To my surprise, we received food that year for one of the holidays (I forget which). Nearly everything we received had her and her friend's name on them!
>
> She can be a pain but also such a blessing! Just thought I'd throw that tidbit to YOU!"
>
> ~Wendy

Learning about Sidewalk makes me love her more, and I believe I love myself a little bit more as well. My friendship with Sidewalk has taught me to care, not just about stuff and things, but life itself, including other people's lives. I see now that the world needs to reconnect with itself. We are all one. If I don't learn to care, I cheat myself and my heart out of living life to the fullest and learning to love others unconditionally.

"Freddy" aka Kurbside Kurby aka Christopher Kerby

Chris Kerby has, at times, been one of my closest friends among the street community. And, as is often the case with many of the street kids, I met him through Sidewalk. For this segment, I will simply refer to him as "Freddy," but he is also known as Kurby.

I introduced myself to Freddy in March of 2016, right around my birthday, which was just a few days before his. At our first meeting, Freddy was a bit skeptical. Without saying a word, Sidewalk need only give him the nod of approval to let him know I was harmless and could be trusted. He warmed up to me right away. I was intrigued because he was personable and had a warmth about him that was different, even refreshing. Freddy is one of the most genuine people I've met in my life. He has a look of Irish descent, adding that to a caring smile; he's a charmer for sure, ladies!

I remember countless examples of Freddy's gentle and kind spirit. He certainly has a passion for protecting those he considers family and will move quickly toward any situation where someone may be in harm's way. He might give a little guy like Bob a verbal warning about considering others' feelings, then go back moments later, kneeling in front of Bob, looking him in the eyes, and putting his hand on Bob's shoulder, gently making sure that he knows that he cares about him as well. Softly telling Bob, he matters and that he is sorry if his words sounded harsh.

I love witnessing these moments. The average person most likely is unaware of these interactions amongst the street community. The family they develop and share, as dysfunctional as it may often appear, but in my 60 plus years of living life, not only experiencing dysfunction and the wounds it has inflicted upon me, but I've witnessed it in other households. It makes the streets look pretty normal to me. The 'untraditionally housed' are just more visible; the rest of us can hide our dysfunction from the world in our homes.

Sometimes I hesitate to do things, such as going out to see a movie, feeling like I should be working on the book, or visiting the street community. But for some reason, the film, *"Solo: A Star Wars Story"* (knowing nothing about the film), called to me. Something inside me kept hinting that it was important I see it; I honestly felt an urgency.

So, one night I hiked it over to the Omnimax Theater, and for seven bucks and two and half hours, my eyes were fixed to the screen, my very soul entranced by the story and the message. The film told the story of Han Solo's youth, with the surprising (for me) revelation that he was a street kid. Scrappy and streetwise, he found hustling to be an acceptable way of life compared to the corrupt societal norms of his planet in that day and age. It was truly the *only* way to survive. Solo didn't buy into the 'Bantha-fodder' his world had to offer but found integrity in looking after his girl and desiring hope for an unimaginable and doubt-filled future.

Solo was one of the hundreds, maybe thousands, disillusioned by the state of the world, the drone of a lifeless society, and deadly oppression. Solo desired something different and hopeful, with an edge of danger and adventure. Solo longed to be armed with purpose.

His heart and spirit speak deeply to the heart and plight of our street youth and what I see in Freddy. He lives for adventure, and like so many others, longs for something new, for purpose, and something worth fighting for. Freddy has the heart of a protector, a warrior, in the eyes of this old guy.

After I learned Freddy's full name, out of curiosity, I began researching the origin of the family name, Kerby. The Kerby's were on a path to freedom from the oppression of a corrupt world.

"To escape the political and religious persecution within England at the time, many English families left for the various British colonies abroad. The voyage was extremely difficult, though, and the cramped, dank ships caused many to arrive in the New World diseased and starving. But for those who made it, the trip was most often worth it. Many of the families who arrived went on to make valuable contributions to the emerging nations of Canada and the United States."

https://www.houseofnames.com

I liken the journey of the Kerby families back in the 17th century to that of Freddy's journey today. And like young Han Solo, disillusioned by a corrupt world, Freddy desires change. It has been extremely difficult for him, but this old guy knows he has a beautiful heart wanting to make a positive impact on our world. For certainly, he has in mine.

One afternoon, I stopped to check in with my street buddies; Leprechaun, Sidewalk, Freddy, and the gang on Third. As I got up from our chat (Freddy wants me to write his biography, but I'm leaning towards a documentary), I said, "I want all you guys to know how much I appreciate your friendship."

Freddy stood up, with a gleam in his eye, he emphatically proclaimed, "Chuck! You are not just our friend; *you are family. I will always have your back. Come here.*" He said this with his arms open wide, then gave me a big hug. Telling someone you'll always have their back, for me, is one of the most honoring and respect-filled promises one person can offer to another on the streets, and Freddy was promising it to me.

Freddy is pictured hard at work, re-finishing a skateboard. He sang while he worked with a beautiful and captivating voice. Rarely do I ever hear him sing, but I stop and listen when he does. He also plays the guitar when he has access to one.

I always look forward to seeing Freddy on the sidewalks downtown. He is one of my safe places. A perfect example of his heart is when I have not seen him for a week or so, realize he is in a group of kids I'm chatting with, then walk over to offer him a sign of respect and honor on the streets, that precious fist-bump. But instead of reciprocating, Freddy will say, "No, Chuck, come here." He'll then put down the skateboard he's sanding or the leather jacket he is patching and stand up with arms open wide. His hugs mean the world to this often-lonely old guy. For, knowing that a man like Freddy trusts and loves a tattered and goofy 60-year-old, a man who has experienced too much loss, failure, and rejection of his own in life, well, it gives me hope. Hope that this world is not completely lost. A world where sidewalks now lead this old guy to the most unexpected and unlikely treasures of all; the loving hearts of the street community.

"Freddy! You big loveable goofball! I will always treasure every one of your Dirty Kid hugs! You are a creative genius! Never forget who you are and where you come from. Han Solo has nothing on you! Love you, man!"

~Poppa Chuck

94

The non-dimmable "Litebulb"

One fall evening when the temperature dropped to an unusual (for Portland) low, Litebulb delighted in showing me how to make a hand-held heater out of tampons and white gas. Yes, TAMPONS!

Litebulb was actually nicknamed 'Dim Litebulb' by a few of the other kids because they thought she wasn't very bright. But that is only because she is often very quiet, intro-spective, and doesn't respond to steer-fodder.

This young street-heart is really very spe-cial. Litebulb is sweet and a bright light for her friends and especially this old guy; always sharing her wisdom, insights, and dry sense of humor. Litebulb journals daily, enjoying the simplicity of life. She is also a protector and encourager.

I've walked alongside Litebulb (with Jeff at times) through some very difficult experiences, as they have with me. On other occasions, we cel-ebrate, like Jeff's birthday in 2020, during the COVID pandemic, in their motel room. We had tacos, nachos, and bur-ritos, along with a huge cheesecake. Litebulb is an integral part of my street family, as well as that of others, and loved dearly by many, like Freddy (as the image shows).

Sitting on the busy sidewalk chatting with me one afternoon, Litebulb pulled out a razor and began touching up her face. She looked up at me matter of factly, stating, "You do what you gotta do out here on the streets."

I love that about Litebulb. She isn't con-cerned about what others think, nor does she live in the darkness of the shaming that is of-

95

ten cast upon her and her friends by some of those in the housed population. She is a beautiful, heartwarming soul… as this old guy's heart sees her.

"I love you dearly, Litebulb. Beyond a shadow of a doubt, you brighten my world each and every time I see you. Never, *EVER*, doubt that!"

~Poppa Chuck

"Hippie Jesus"

Poppa Chuck: *"Jesus, why do you hang out with an old guy like me?"*
Jesus: *"Chuck, everyone needs love."*

This dude's eyes are a freakin' beautiful blue. You may not realize it at the moment, but Hippie or Jesus (whichever one prefers to call him) is the 'When Sidewalks Smile' cover kid. His profile is double-exposed with a photo taken of a lamppost in Waterfront Park.

While taking the Waterfront photo of a lamppost with a new phone, I positioned myself so that the morning sun shone through the globe. A few days earlier, I had randomly taken photos of Jesus. While reviewing my photos from that past week, I began experimenting with the new photoshop double exposure feature. When I took the photos of Jesus, I had little hope they would turn out well. But they were far more remarkable than I could have imagined. So, I decided to use the photos of Jesus to play with that double exposure feature. During the process, I positioned Jesus' eye in the middle of the globe of the lamppost with the sun shining through. Nothing was planned. And such is this book's cover story and a metaphor for the *light* this young man brings to the sidewalks of my world.

Each week on Sunday, under the Hawthorne Bridge on the east side of the Willamette River, a meal is provided for the homeless. I often go so

I can visit and check in on some of my street buddies. One Sunday, Litebulb, Jesus, Jeff, and I were having a good time. It was a time of laughter and friendship. I took the time to update my friends on the progress of the book, showing them new photos and letting Litebulb read the lead-in to the segment about her.

But our laughter was interrupted when an angry man entered the scene just after Jeff had gone to use a restroom. I was about to experience something that moved my heart to new levels of appreciation for my friends. While he was gone, for some bizarre reason, a man with a thick accent demanded that a park bench be cleaned off and pointed at me in a threatening manner.

"I don't understand," I said to Jesus with anxiety and PTSD beginning to kick in. I glanced at Jesus, not wanting to take my eyes off this guy in case he came at me. He seemed infuriated.

"It's my dinner, and those are my bags," Jesus said to me, sounding confused. He could tell I was emotionally struggling with the situation.

"That is my lunch, and those are my things! Why should he clean it up?" Jesus told him, contradicting the man.

"No!" The man pointed at me, then commanded. "You clean it up!" his anger now escalating, his eyes fixed on me as he stood maybe eight feet away at the most, fiercely glaring at me with fists clenched.

I was confused at first, thinking I had missed something or had done something wrong. This is usually the case whenever someone is angry with me. Jesus simply said to me, "He woke me up in the middle of the night last night on the other side of the river. I'm not sure what his problem is." Jesus is a trained Marine. He didn't take his eyes off of the man. He watched him carefully.

I wasn't sure what to do. My anxiety increased. This man was much younger and brawny. Inwardly, I was concerned he was going to attack me. I stayed quiet.

The man then walked over to the bench, pacing back and forth, becoming more agitated and looking in our direction. At that moment, Jesus took charge. It was like Jesus' small 5'4" frame had become a powerhouse of strength. Stomping over to the man, he got in his face and strongly demanded that he stop. I'd never seen Jesus being anything more than docile. He had to push the man away with his whole body several times.

I noticed Litebulb in my peripheral vision opening her backpack sitting on the ground. I didn't think she noticed what was going on. Then I said to her, "Jesus is protecting me."

"I know," she said, pulling the biggest crescent wrench I've ever seen out of her backpack. I didn't understand at that moment, but she too was preparing to defend her friends, Jesus and me. Then, the man actually stopped; he got the message and walked away. Jesus, along with Litebulb, came to my rescue. It was all over in the blink of an eye. I marveled at their willingness to protect me.

To lighten the mood, Litebulb told me I needed to video Jeff juggling. "What? Jeff can juggle? Why did I not know this?"

"Yup. And he's pretty damn good at it," she said proudly.

With the meal now over, we all prepared to leave. I needed to go home and get to work. Writing this adventure would be one of my tasks. But as packs were getting strapped onto our backs and we got the area tidied up, and Jesus took his plate of food off the bench to take with him, an older gentleman with long gray hair, looking tired and broken, walked up to us.

With a weak voice, he asked us, "Are they still serving lunch?"

"Sorry, man. They were done a while ago. They've already left," Jeff explained, apologizing to the man.

Without hesitation, Jesus walked up to him with his plate of food, "Here, you can have this," he offered the man. On the plate were a delicious open-faced sloppy joe, a green salad with ranch dressing, and two chocolate chip cookies. The man was very grateful, as was I, for my friends and their amazing hearts.

Over the years I've known Jesus, he has always stopped to chat with me on the sidewalks of Fourth Street, where he spends most of his days hanging out with friends. On other occasions, he has taken me on walks through a nearby park sharing stories about his adventures on the streets. And sometimes, he simply hangs out at my place.

Jesus never asks for anything. When I offer him help (buying him a coffee or maybe giving him a few bucks now and then), he is always surprised, offering me a humble and grateful smile in return.

"I love you, Hippie Jesus! Your friendship and concern for this old guy's welfare are GREATLY appreciated! And thank you for loving me."

~Poppa Chuck

Now, with a whole family of Dirty Kids welcoming me into their lives, life was becoming magical. Yet, Love was taking me deeper into a realm of compassion and unconditional love that began to change me, giving me purpose in life; offering hope to the hopeless.

Chapter Six

"I Do Not Exist!":
"A Plea for a Love that Encompasses All"

I Do NOT Exist!" By Violet Fae Rabbitt

Sky blue,
so, I got a clue,
everything is really opposite and upside down,
hanged man above the ground,
vibrating,
I create the sound,
I ride the waves until they matter,

created time and space as they shattered,
pick up the pieces,
I'm leaving crumbs,
I'm as lost as the forest reaches,
following the hums
my soul's drums,

sacred fool,
I just jumped off the cliff,
hidden jewel,
I'm your new favorite myth.

"Miranda Wrong"

~as lived by Raquel Raven McKenzie Pendleton

People: *"What do you carry around in that huge backpack?"*
Raquel: ***"Trauma!"***

I sat, joyfully chatting with my new street-hearts, Raquel and Violet, for a bit in the fall of 2018. Our intimate conversation began one afternoon when I passed by them, sitting on a sidewalk. As I nodded a respectful hello, Raquel announced, "You look like you need a hug!"

"Yes, please!" I said, feeling very honored. I spoke into her ear during that hug and promised her, "I will hug you anytime...no matter where." This was not something I've said to anyone before, and never since, to my recollection. I knew this promise was meant just for Raquel.

I sat down on the sidewalk with my new friends. We began to chat about life, with me all the while attempting to avoid the poo on the sidewalk, which was actually a piece of cardboard with the word "poop" hilariously written on it with a thick black magic marker.

We soon began revealing our struggles, weaknesses, and our common desire for a world filled with a love that encompasses all. Raquel then sang for me as she played an old-fashioned washboard. It was moving and raw, describing the plight of an alcoholic and drug addict in the first person and the trauma experienced by someone who is *different*. I was immobilized by the pain, suffering, and the message that much of the world only sees Raquel and others like her as nothing more than trash or a problem that needs to be fixed. My new friend let me capture this on video, which I then uploaded to YouTube.

Raquel Raven McKenzie Pendleton (Cover)

"We Are All Compost in Training"
Written by Ramshackle Glory

https://youtu.be/oz-GdxY6FEo

Raquel's story speaks from the hearts of every person, young and old, who is trapped in a world where they are not allowed to be themselves (hence the pseudonym, "Miranda Wrong"). These individuals most often experience brutal emotional and verbal abuse at the hands of their peers, loved ones, and the world around them as a whole. I know this truth all too well.

In addition, please take a moment to experience their world through a profound and thought-provoking song and video by *Wrabel*. Get out the tissues; although the message is heartbreaking, there is an essence of hope and love waiting in the wings.

"The Village"

https://youtu.be/tilsrO-3gcQ

On a Wednesday morning, Raquel posted on a social network, indicating that she was distraught and in a desperate mental health crisis. Certainly, and without pause, this old guy posted loving support. Along with that and the posts of support and love from others was a heartbreaking post from her mom in California. Vickie shared her love for Raquel but expressed her distress; that she could not be there in person to love and hold her daughter, which broke my heart.

Hating that I could do no more, I signed off of my computer to attend to the many appointments on my schedule for the day. Fortunately, each of the appointments is in the heart of downtown Portland where I frequently come across a street kid or two that I can touch bases with and let them know they matter to me.

On my way to visit my mental health provider, I noticed a person sitting on the curb at the corner of a popular intersection where the kids hang out during the warm weather. They were alone, though, seeming to be oblivious to the world around them as they feverishly wrote in what appeared to be a journal. I love to write, so I always notice a fellow writer and take a moment to encourage them. As I drew nearer, I realized it was Raquel!

I quietly walked around a lamppost, not wanting to startle nor disturb her. I slowly knelt to sit at Raquel's side. "Hello, sweetheart," I softly said to her.

She raised her head slowly to see who was there to sit with her. When her eyes met mine, I saw a pain-filled sadness that nearly broke my heart. Without words, Raquel then laid her head on my shoulder, my cheek resting on the top of her head, my arm around her shoulders. But more importantly, I held her heart in my own.

After a few moments of silence, I gently said, "This hug is from your mom as well. When she saw your post on Facebook this morning, she was sad that she couldn't be here to hold you. So, this hug is from your mom. I'm holding you, for her. She loves you so very much, Raquel."

"Yes, she does," Raquel whispered. Then she straightened up and returned to looking at her journal. "I was just working on this poem." Her sadness came through each word she spoke.

"I love your poems, Raquel. I want to put some of your work in the book. There was one poem you posted a couple of weeks ago that I found to be exceptional." Raquel then turned the pages of her notebook until she found the exact poem I referred to.

"Yes, that's it. May I put that one in the book?"

"Yes, of course," she replied.

I then explained to her, "At some point, I will need a release signed by you with permission to include that in your story."

With that said, Raquel turned to a blank page in the notebook, scribbled a note providing me with permission, and signed it "Raquel

Raven McKenzie Pendleton." I was moved by her heart to participate in the When Sidewalks Smile Project and grateful for her willingness to put herself out there in the midst of her own pain and suffering, as well as the many challenges she faces in her daily life.

Holding that handwritten note now in my hand felt like someone had just handed me a million bucks. Then I asked if I could take a photo of the poem in her journal. As soon as I took the photos, the blaring sound of automobile horns distracted us from our conversation. There was a commotion taking place out in the intersection. "Hey, you!" Raquel cried out as she quickly stood up, looking intently into the center of the intersection.

I stood up as well. Gutter was crossing the intersection looking haggard and lost.

"Gutter!" I shouted along with Raquel as the two of us instinctively walked out into traffic to rescue our friend. With Raquel on Gutter's left side and this old guy on his right, we helped him to the sidewalk safely.

"Are you okay?" we asked.

"No. I just got out of the hospital. I'm so hungry. Do you have anything to drink?" he asked in a dull, desperate tone.

Raquel immediately grabbed her drink, handing it to Gutter. He guzzled long and deep from the soda bottle. I realized at this moment that Gutter shouldn't be alone in his current condition. I wondered if I was going to be late to my appointment, which was nearby, but for me, Gutter was more important. He needed to eat and a spot to rest.

Suddenly, and with compassion, Raquel took charge. "I've got food stamps. I'll take care of you."

I was touched by the fact that Raquel, in her own pain, was now caring for another who was also hurting. She looked past her own need to provide for the needs of our dear friend. "So, you got this, Raquel?" I asked.

"Yes," was her confident reply.

"Okay," I said, feeling the pride of a father. "I need to get to an appointment. You two take really good care. I'll come back and check on you afterward." Looking into Raquel's eyes, I said, "Thank you for taking care of Gutter. I love you, sweetheart." I waited for the Walk sign to change at the crosswalk and continued on my journey, knowing that both of my friends were safe. I was grateful for the love and compassion of one hurting Dirty Kid for another.

The following is the poem I asked Raquel if I could include in this project. I am in awe of her deep connection with her heart and the profound way she communicates her heartbreaking, very real, and raw truths.

Crying in my hands

Barely can stand
Bleeding from my heart
A person you can't stand
You can't see me as you pass on the streets
URCHIN. Lost cause!
Cause,
Fuck social norms
I'm blending at the source
Snorting life left nostril feeling remorse
Of course,
bad habit
Drink, eat, shit, repeat
Concrete trapped around my feet
DROWNING
I'm making sounds at the surface,
blurting out obscenities that are real to me
but the average person couldn't see.
Just a me trying to freely be me
WRONG
I do have rights,
stand up to fight
My wrist bleeding.
Am I doing this right?

Here in Raquel's story, I think about how the Dirty Kids and buskers sing and lament on the sidewalks of downtown Portland. I often take note that no one appears to be listening to their profound messages. Rarely do I see anyone stop and take note of the hearts of these kids because they are too busy judging them. Nor do they hear the message of unconditional love that eludes our dying world.

I am reminded of the words spoken by one of my favorite love heroes, his message to a deaf, violent, and heartless people, raiding his Kingdom of Love:

"To what can I compare this generation? They are like children sitting in the marketplaces and calling out to others: 'We played the pipe for you, and you did not dance; we sang a dirge, and you did not mourn.'"

~Yeshua of Nasrath

I have to ask myself countless times as I learn more about the buskers; "Am I listening? Do I have ears to hear the message crying out to us? A song declaring the need for unconditional love sung to this world by our society's outcasts? Do I care about others? Do I?"

Raquel now has her own apartment near downtown's waterfront. She is happy and very much in love with her fiancé, Ocean. They have created their own band, "The Ports of Streetland." The two are making recordings and videos. My favorite is a cover of 357 String Band's "Black River Blues."

The Ports of Streetland / (Cover) Black River Blues

https://youtu.be/bxxJf_hgb10

"I love you, Raquel, my sweet street-heart. And I so love that you affectionately call me 'Pops.' Thank you for teaching me that loving the unloved of this world is far more valuable than judging them. You will always have my love... anytime... no matter where."

~Pops

The following song is a favorite of the kids, reflecting the heart of many of the outcasts of society, who see themselves as mistakes and believe the world would be better off without them.

Misanthropic Drunken Loner [Official Music Video]

Days N Daze /   **https://youtu.be/v0dUnoecoZ0**

"A heart is not measured by how much YOU love, but by how much YOU are loved by others."

L. Frank Baum, "The Wizard of Oz"

"gutter"~The Beloved

Wild, on the wind you ride,
Wise, in the heart, abide
Wanderer, at my side
Wodan draw near ...

By Nathan Shrader, aka "gutter-slut"

Nathan's street name is not capitalized in the title because he sees himself as nothing more than gutter-trash. But for the sake of readability and flow, I will refer to Nathan simply as *Gutter* throughout the text.

As I started writing about my experiences and compiling these stories, I especially wanted to include Gutter in this book. I hoped we would connect on some level in the near future. I desired to learn about the heart of this Dirty Kid, hoping to connect with Gutter ever since Sidewalk mentioned his name and shared that he was her street brother. She talked about him often, and all of the kids know him, but it was Sidewalk Sarah's heart for Gutter that intrigued me the most. I, too, wanted to get to know him in time.

My only interactions with Gutter for two years were usually seeing him sitting alone on a sidewalk, very quiet, and always appearing to be sad.

Gutter never seemed like he wanted to talk. I always honored that, giving him space. But those two years went by, and still, I had no connection with him. Then, upon his release from jail in the winter of 2019, a story worth telling began to unfold as I came to learn something I didn't see coming about this seemingly quiet young man. I'd last seen Gutter on Third just a few short weeks before his arrest. It was the time when I'd left him in the capable hands of Raquel on a street corner while she was in her own distress. With Raquel's obvious caring heart and concern for Gutter, I was even more curious. I was asking myself, *"What is it about Gutter that makes all of these street kids love him so much?"*

It was over a period of several weeks, beginning in December of 2018, while he was jailed for an exaggerated assault charge, that I began to witness the love of the street community pouring out for Gutter.

I attended Gutter's court dates in support of him and on behalf of his mother, 'Mama Kat' (as the Dirty Kids call her). She and I had met through Sidewalk on a social network. Mama Kat lived 3,000 miles away and was unable to attend the court appearances. I can't sit back and let the kids go through these difficult life experiences on their own. I ended up learning something really special through the experience of supporting Gutter. I began to witness the hearts of the street community sending well wishes and love to him, either through his mom or myself. It was remarkable, the outpouring of love for their beloved friend. I was both moved deeply and intrigued every time one of the kids said, *"Please tell Gutter I love him."*

Gutter's mom sent me a message from Massachusetts shortly after he was arrested, which caused me to take a step back and listen to these kids' hearts. Mama Kat wrote: "One boy just called me crying his eyes out. He wants to go steal Gutter and bring him home. Bless his heart."

He and I began communicating during his time in jail. In the beginning, I'd travel to the Justice Center in downtown Portland or the Inverness Jail facility out in NE Portland, leaving handwritten messages for him. It was in those simple notes to Gutter that I told him about all his street buddy's love for him. In my notes, I wrote down each street kid's name. I felt as though I experienced the love the kids have for Gutter flowing in and through me, out to him. With every message passed along to me from the streets and sidewalks of downtown Portland, I was becoming more curious about the love they all held deeply for their friend. Especially Sidewalk Sarah in particular. She insisted I share these words with him, *"Tell Gutter I love him MEGA dog bones!"*

A few weeks later, through his mother (Mama Kat), I was to learn how important that message was and the depth of its meaning; an endearing 'insiders' message of love and support. It took several of those handwritten notes, but most of all, it took his mom assuring him I was a good guy, only wanting to support him. One day, to my surprise and delight, I got a call from Gutter. In that first phone conversation, although Gutter didn't talk much and sounded very sad, I made it a point to let him know how profound the love from all of his friends was to me. I learned, at that moment, that Gutter was hesitant to believe it.

During one phone conversation (I looked forward to every one of them), I let Gutter know that upon his release, he could stay with me temporarily, at least until he got a bed in one of the shelter programs. I could also walk alongside him in approaching and navigating the healthcare systems. Gutter still did not know me as well as his friends do. He just knew me as the old guy writing a book who had taken the time to support him while he was in jail. He did not yet trust me, which was fine. I was more interested in Gutter knowing I respected him and was not going to tell him what to do. I would simply be there for him.

Over three months, I attended four court appearances in support of Gutter. In the last appearance, the original charges were reduced significantly. I was surprised and overjoyed during the court session to hear the judge's decision to release him that evening.

I left the courthouse happy and relieved but concerned if Gutter may not have a place to stay that night and whether he could meet all the requirements of his 36 months of parole. I shared the good news and also expressed this concern in a text message to his mom. Having a seizure disorder coupled with mental and physical health issues makes daily life a challenge for Gutter. A life that is even more difficult and nearly impossible to navigate on his own, let alone while living on the streets.

I had only walked half a block from the courthouse when I unexpectedly came across Dirty Jeff in that cold weather. He stood at the entrance to a shop that was no longer in business on Fourth. He was shivering and trying to keep warm. He is one of Gutter's best friends. I had no clue, in this chance meeting with Jeff, that I was going to learn one of the many reasons why all of his street buddies love Gutter so much. As we began to chat, I noticed his eyes were exceptionally blue, like fiercely blue, if there is such a color called 'fierce blue.' I was driven to comment on it, "Dang, Jeff, your eyes are really blue today!"

With an impish grin, Jeff informed me, "I'm not stoned, that's why! There's probably not as much of my pupil showing, so you can see more of the color today."

I laughed at Jeff's always witty sense of humor and then announced, "Gutter got released. I just came from the courthouse."

Jeff's eyes lit up, becoming even brighter and bluer. "That's so awesome!" Jeff said. I then explained to him the stipulations of Gutter's parole and release.

Jeff then got a serious look on his face, "So, Chuck, what you're saying is, we gotta all help keep him on track."

I thought to myself, "Wow, these were certainly words coming from the heart of a devoted friend, echoing that of others as well." Then, at that moment, the mystery of why Gutter is so loved by the street community began to unfold.

My heart now deeply moved by Jeff and remembering all of his friends' hearts for Gutter, I said, "You mean, you and the other kids… you would do that for him?"

"Oh, hell yeah, we will," Jeff proclaimed.

Just then, my cell phone went off. I looked at it to find Sidewalk was calling me. I was already moved by Jeff's heart for Gutter; it wasn't surprising that Sidewalk was chiming in.

"Sorry Jeff, I gotta take this. I'll make it quick," I said, showing him the phone, which simply read, "Sidewalk Calling."

"It's okay," Jeff smiled with that always easygoing charm of his. "I understand."

"Hey, Sidewalk, Gutter's out." With delight, she explained that Mama Kat had just called from Massachusetts with the news.

Sidewalk then took charge, "If he calls you, cause he doesn't have my number, tell him he has a room for the night at a motel."

"Wow, Sidewalk. So, you'll look after him tonight?"

"Yes, of course. He's all set up for the night. I'll go to meet him when he gets out of the courthouse. I'll show up at 8:00, but I know he may not be out till 9:00. I'll just wait for him."

"Thank you, sweetheart," I said. "You guys are *AMAZING!*"

Sidewalk reassured me that he'd be okay. "Thank you for everything, Chuck. You know we love you."

"I love you too, Sidewalk." I hung up and turned to Jeff, "What is it, Jeff?!" I cried out with a bit of emotion and tears welling up. ***WHAT IS THE REASON THAT ALL YOU KIDS LOVE Gutter the most, it seems, more than all the other kids?"***

"*YOU DON'T KNOW?*" Jeff asked me with surprise.

"NO ...know what? What is it, Jeff?" And here part of the mystery, revealed, falling right into my lap, spoken to me, from my street buddy's heart.

"I love him because he saved my life," Jeff said, looking me straight in the eye. "He literally saved me from getting killed twice and another time from alcohol poisoning!"

"What? How? What happened?" I begged him.

"One time -" Jeff explained, "- someone was going to kill me, literally! Gutter took him down; he saved my life. And another time, he punched me in the gut when I had alcohol poisoning. I vomited all the alcohol. So, here I am today, and now I never touch a drop."

So, there it was. The mystery finally unraveling about our beloved Gutter; what I'd been hoping to learn and understand for so long about this quiet and nearly always sad appearing young man. For, in hearing that Gutter had saved the life of someone like Jeff, a good guy who has been there for me during some of my difficult bouts with depression and the environmental oppression where I lived, well, I was a very grateful old guy. As I began to process the truth I'd just learned about our beloved Gutter, I realized, "Jeff is alive because of Mama Kat's son." I wondered how many others Gutter had protected and looked after.

Further proving my point about the love in the street community for Gutter, his mom shared with me that a young man named Taylor came out to Oregon from Massachusetts not long after their best friend Lynus died. Taylor, aka TaylorMade, told Mama Kat he knew in his heart of hearts that he was supposed to travel across the U.S. to look after Gutter. A beautiful sentiment in this old guy's eyes!

The treasures hidden behind these Dirty Kids' facial tattoos, wild, colorful mohawks, and worn out, patched up, and tattered coveralls; will surprise and delight anyone willing to look beyond what they think they see into the beauty of the hearts within. Just as it was, and is, for this old guy, the mystery of one more street-heart, revealed. These kids are amazing! I grow and learn to love them more and more every day.

I learned one of the many funny stories told about Gutter through a social network chat. Patty shared with me one day, *"I knew Gutter from back in high school when his mom lived on the border of Northampton and Holyoke, Massachusetts. I was a freshman when Gutter had a combination padlock stuck and locked in his earlobe because he didn't have the code."*

Another great story I learned on the sidewalk of Third in March of 2019. Chatting with Sidewalk, Gutter, and a few of their friends one afternoon, Sidewalk announced, "OH!! You just have to put the 'Milk-Bone Dog Biscuits' story in the book!" Gutter then tells me that at the age of seven, he began eating dog biscuits. He really liked them. Sidewalk and the kids all laughed while reminding Gutter to tell the whole tale. He dipped Milk-Bone dog biscuits in peanut butter, eating them by the box. Gutter chuckled and admitted it was certainly a true story and not one that he regrets nor is ashamed of. [Author's note: KIDS: Don't do this at home!]

Anytime I am on the sidewalks of downtown, and I come across my good buddy, Gutter, he gives me a big, warm hug. In those moments, I offer him my cell phone so that he could call his mom. Gutter's heart for his mom is reflected in his concern for her health and liver problems. Mama Kat shared with me that he called her from jail a few years back, gently offering her this advice, *"Mom, maybe you shouldn't drink alcohol at all, so you don't get sick."*

Gutter's Heart: My Son, My Only Child

As told to Poppa Chuck by Mama Kat (content has been lightly edited for clarity). *"As early as three months old, I could see his intelligence and willingness to help. We were living with my parents; they had just bought a new home. We had to stay in an apartment for a few months while the tenant living in their new home lived out her lease. There were new carpets. The fuzz balls from the carpet were all over the place. My little baby watched me pick up the fuzz balls from the rugs. I did this so he wouldn't stick them in his mouth.*

One day, he started crawling. As he made his way across the rug and came across a fuzzball, he picked it up in his hand, then crawled over to the trash can. That is when he began to squat because he wanted to place it inside the trash can. He was the most awesome baby. He never cried; he was a VERY smart and strong little guy. My mother swore he had an iron grip when he grabbed your fingers.

As he grew, he began to walk and talk, and he was the absolute light of my life. He was fun, adorable, and so kind-hearted. He was the funniest little kid. He lived with my parents for a while, and he told my stepfather one day, 'Grandpa, when you die, I'm not going to let them bury you.' To which Kat's stepfather replied, 'Well, what are you going to do with me?'

Nathan replied, 'I'm going to drive you around in your truck.' (Nathan said that because Kat's dad took her everywhere in his truck).

That boy was cute as could be!

He would share whatever he had with his friends, not denying them anything he had. And again, his intelligence showed. He went to school every day just like any other child, and I promised him five dollars for every 'A' he received. His generosity, his sense of humor, and the way he mocked my facial expressions blew my mind.

After a time, my parents had him with them. They moved to a city called Westfield, a decision I was very uneasy with, but I allowed it. As a teenager, Nathan began sleeping downtown so he would be near his girlfriend. He would sleep behind dumpsters and laundromats for warmth. My stepdad had to lure him home so he'd get some rest. But his heart never changed, ALWAYS kind and generous as ever.

After a time, my mother became ill, my stepfather had been placed in a nursing home, and it was time for Gutter to come home and live with me. He began drinking at age fifteen, doing drugs, getting into trouble, going to court. Court day became a regular event in our home. I wanted him to join the Job Corps, he refused, saying that it would be like getting locked up.

I love my son with all my heart. I always tell him he's my 'guts,' hence the name 'Gutter.' I tell him, "Mega dog bones," because, when he was small, I would ask him, "How much do I love you?"

And Nathan would ask, "How much?"

I would outstretch my arms and say,
"MEGA DOG BONES!"

When he was about sixteen years old, he started calling himself 'Gutter [slut]' because he slept in the gutter and wouldn't come home.

Gutter made friends easily. I enrolled him in Holyoke High School, and after four years as a freshman, I got him a job working in one of my bosses' restaurants doing dishes.

He did not like it. Gutter spent less and less time with me and kept skipping school, telling me, "I'm going to Westfield to be with my friends." Then, for weeks at a time, he would not come home.

I was working two jobs to support us, and he would bring kids home to me that he would find on the street. Two of them lived next door in an apartment complex. When I came home from work one night at 11 pm, he had those two children in my home. Gutter asked me if they could stay for a while because their parents went out to a bar, and they had no electricity. Of course, I said, "Yes." And that's where it began, with meeting 'Dirty Kids.'

The day I met his best friend, Lynus, I was staying in a cellar apartment on the river in East Hampton. It was Gutter's 20th birthday. I knew he would be around for his birthday gift. There was a knock at the door. When I opened it, I found him and Lynus standing on my doorstep. I asked Gutter where they had come from? He said they'd spent the night on the beach with a small fire, just hanging out, telling me they had waited till morning, not wanting to wake us. Gutter asked if Lynus could spend the day.

Lynus was homeless, sweet, and quiet. It was October 10th and warm out that morning, but not yet hot. I told Gutter, "Of course, Lynus can stay." Later we had dinner and cake and took a ride into town. Gutter wanted a beer. We returned to my home; he and his friend spent the night, filled their bellies, and refused showers. This was the start of the whole 'Dirty Kid' thing.

After that came more and more kids Gutter would find on the streets. Though he did not know them well, he would bring some home to me in the dead of winter for a warm place to sleep and a hot meal. Back then, I worked at Amherst College. I would get off work at 2 am. There were times I came home to a house full of kids because the snow was flying and the wind was blowing. There were female friends, male friends, and dogs. Gutter always knew that if he brought them home, I would feed them and let them get warm for the night and then possibly get a ride into town the next morning, where they would do their 'thing.' But sadly, Gutter would still refuse to stay with me.

I moved out of that cellar apartment to a house in Hadley. One night I came home from work. I worked at a very prestigious college until two am in those days, doing food service for the students. Gutter had a young man named Jace with him. They showed up while I was at work. My ex-husband let them in. When I got home from work, they were baking fish sticks and cooking some other things to eat.

They all became part of my family, maybe since I could no longer have children. So, so many kids have touched my heart. They called me Mama Kat. I fell in love with ALL of them. I came home one evening, well morning, at 2 am. My husband was freaking out because Gutter brought a bunch of Dirty Kids home. I didn't even see them when I came into the yard. They were all in sleeping bags out there. I didn't count, but there were many. I told my ex-husband, "Be quiet, they're just passing through." I learned that they had just jumped off a train, in need of rest, and a good meal.

Gutter knew that day that I was not angry, but his heart was so generous, and he continued to bring Dirty Kids to me when he would find them on the street—always sharing and knowing that I would feed them and let them stay the night.

Seeing [experiencing firsthand] Gutter's generosity and his kindness extremely impressed upon my soul. He went to jail for some stupid thing and was on work release. I was fighting for my disability at the time, and my son sent me money from jail to help me out. He was, and still is, the light of my life and OWNS MY HEART.

Once I was awarded disability, I went to court with Gutter regarding his release from jail. He told the court his mother was ill, and he wanted to take care of her. They released him on that condition. At this point, he took off and never said 'goodbye.' I would get calls from all over the country, hospital after hospital, contacted me on his way out to Oregon. He was self-medicating heavily. It was a rough trip for him.

Gutter would always call his Mommy. To this day, he calls me Mommy. He thanks me for loving his Dirty Kids and thanks me for loving him.

So, I ask you, how could I NOT love such a kind and generous soul? My one and only child. I miss him with an intensity no one else can understand. He gave me a grandson. He is a beautiful boy who looks very much like him. I adore this child too. I am in touch with Gutter and fear for my son every day. This is what he chose [the life of a Dirty Kid]. This is what he wanted. Another day goes by, and with each day, I would give anything to hear that knock on the door, then hear Gutter call out, "Mommy!" At 35 years old, he still calls me Mommy. Lynus called me Mum. The rest of the kids call me Mama Kat. There are still some of the kids around here, and they still check on me, always kind and loving; some grew up, some did not.

Gutter called me the other day, "Hi Mommy," he said. "I love you."

"Hello, son. I love you too," I replied.

I do not know what made him choose this path, BUT I DO KNOW my son is one of THE MOST kind and caring people I know. He calls me on his favorite holidays, telling me he misses me.

I don't know if he understands how much I miss him and want to be near him and my grandson. But I'll tell the world that no matter what, he is my heart. And when I cry, he cries. And when he cries, I cry. This is something that will never ever change.

So, people, if you see a 'Dirty Kid' with tattoos and the smell of homelessness, try to understand then they all have a soul, and they are not all bad kids. I know this first-hand, and I love them all! You have to look BEYOND what you see visually to really understand them. I have to add, with all the Dirty Kids that passed through my home and my life, not one of them ever disrespected, stole from me, or made me uncomfortable. That is why I call them my kids. We could all learn from them [the Dirty Kids and Travelers]. It saddens me that society looks down on them like pieces of poop. I hope this book sells and opens people's eyes.

I expect to hear from him on Easter [unless] he's locked up. Fingers crossed. He promised he would call, and I always taught him that a promise is forever."

~Mama Kat

This old guy would like to add after Gutter was released from jail, I ran into him on the streets more often. He was no longer sitting on a curb, appearing to be sad. One of those times, he happily declared himself to be the most loved kid on the streets. And, *EVERY TIME* he sees me, he gives me that big, very welcome hug.

Yes, I **MUST** agree with Mama Kat; I am very grateful my eyes have been opened to see the beauty in all these Dirty Kids, like Gutter. Peering into the amazing hearts of the kids, well, it's the gift of a lifetime!

"I love you, Gutter. Thank you for letting me in and for all your amazing hugs!"

~Poppa Chuck

"Leprechaun" aka Benjamin Thompson

One morning I stopped to chat with the kids on Third. Freddy was sanding a skateboard, so I thought it a good opportunity to take a few photos. "Hey, Freddy." I asked him as I knelt down next to him on the curb, "Do you mind if I take a few photos for the book?"

"Sure," he said, continuing to focus on his task. While I took the photos, he turned to Leprechaun, who was lounging on the sidewalk with his hands behind his head.

"Leprechaun," Freddy announced, "Let Chuck take a few photos of you for the book."

It makes me proud that Freddy promotes the project within the Dirty Kid community. But even more so, I was intrigued when Leprechaun told me, "I've got one helluva story."

This made me curious, but I had no clue that two years later, I'd be blown away by the depth of Ben's honesty, insights, self-awareness, and love for life. The following are Ben's own words with very little editing for clarity.

"Life on the streets had plenty of hardship. I was faced with all the struggles everyone else does, such as dealing with the view of the world around you and dealing with how society treats you. I've always tried to model the attitude of those that were doing well. I never wanted to seem weak or needful.

There've been plenty of nights where I've been alone and cold, curled up under a bridge or in a doorway in the rain without even so much as a blanket. I have never forgotten what it feels like; for the tips of your fingers and toes to be completely numb, yet at the same time, they're burning like fire because of the cold outside. To this day, I still say there's no better feeling than fresh socks, new clothes, and getting to take a shower after weeks of going without one. Those are still the three best feelings in the world to me.

Leprechaun was my name, and it's what everybody knew me by. But the longer it went on, the more it felt like a character. In some ways, I miss that character part of me now because Leprechaun would do things that Ben would think twice about. Leprechaun always had the perfect come-back loaded when people started to get witty.

Leprechaun was everything I had to be at that time to survive. Leprechaun was ingratiated by the respect of others. I felt I mattered and was feared or treated with hesitancy by the ones that meant nothing to me. Being the small dude I am, it felt great.

I've met people ranging from train-hoppers like Sidewalk and Freddy to the home bums like Hippie Jesus and Dirty Jeff. I've met doctors who have given up their practices, gang members who spent most of their life in prison. I've met mothers and fathers who have, for reasons unbeknownst to me, come to be in the same spot as I am.

For some reason, it didn't matter who they were; most people felt comfortable talking to me. People would come to me with their problems, and at the time, they would tell me that I had just the right words for them. Or I told them exactly what they needed to hear for the better. It was nice feeling needed by people. I don't know why I craved this feeling so much. It's a feeling to this day I can't help but yearn for. People would tell me how much wisdom I have and how much of a positive impact I made on their lives.

Street kids would come to me seeking some kind of council in one form or another, whether it was handling their own street vendetta's and how they should go about it or helping people deal with the loss of loved ones.

The stuff that grieved me the most was assessing my own standing in life. I love the streets, and I love all my friends. But then there was the fatigue of it all. It was draining me. It weighed heavily on the condition of my health. At one point, I went a long time without the glasses that were the correct prescription, causing vision problems. I started getting sick a lot. I got body lice,

121

scabies, and other parasites. I would go to the hospitals and get sent away with little to no treatment based on the fact that I was a transient.

If a yuppie talked to me, the only thing they wanted to talk about was my homelessness, how I got to be homeless, what it's like being homeless, and why I don't do anything to change it. And that's all they ever wanted to know. The repetitiveness of it was driving me mad. It was all anybody ever wanted to know about me.

People wanted to know why I was smiling and happy while I was on the corner of 7-Eleven with no shoes on, hanging out with people, flying a sign. There's been a couple of times I asked them, "Don't you laugh when you're hanging out with your friends?"

Now that I'm inside [a single parent raising my 2-year-old son, Zephyrus], I have a story that speaks of recovery. I don't even really like to call it recovery. Because that's not what it feels like, it just feels like the next chapter. It's not easy, but I'm doing my best day by day. I'm just going to do right by my son."

– Ben Thompson

"By the way, Ben, what is your age?" I asked as we ended the interview. I thought he must be older than he looks.

"I'm 23 now," he replied.

Shocked and thinking he must have hit the wrong key on the keyboard, I asked, ***"You're only 23???"***

"Yep, I'm only 23. Crazy, ain't it?"

Street youth tell it like it is. No pretense or self-shaming is on Ben's agenda, as he shares his story and heart with me. And without hesitation or reservation, sharing his truth with this old guy is an eye-opening opportunity to gain an understanding of the hearts and lives of others, rather than condemning them. Maybe if we simply listen with ears wide open, rather than with an agenda, we may begin to learn ...how to love.

The second edition of When Sidewalks Smile will delve into Leprechaun's amazing insights into the street-wise Leprechaun and his soul-journey into becoming Ben, a man of integrity and profound self-awareness!

Ben! Thank you so much for contributing to the When Sidewalks Smile series. You blow me away, dude! I could read a whole book just of you sharing your life, truths, and insights. No matter how dark they may appear to be, you are a light, dude! Always know that! The world needs more Ben's. I love you like a grandson!

~Poppa Chuck

Meeting the outcasts of our world and developing intimate friendships with so many in the street community, led me further into opening myself up to unexpected and precious encounters everywhere I went in downtown Portland. I was soon to learn love was everywhere when I gave myself to being present and loving others, even from my own wounds.

Chapter Seven

"Beautiful, Magical, and Precious Sidewalk Moments"

Bebopp 9/2018

Bebopp

Many of society's outcasts are but 'ghosts' in downtown Portland, scarcely noticed by anyone except their own. Little did I realize, until I met this young man, that a message was offered to me through the outcasts. Like my street buddy, 'Bebopp,' with a magic marker in hand, using his very clothing to send a message to the world.

I took a liking to Bebopp from the get-go. A gentle and sweet soul, my new friend is quite the character and very friendly. He complimented me on my new tie-dyed t-shirt during our introductions.

"It's the first one I've made since I was a kid," I explained a bit timidly. "You really like this?"

"Yes!" Bebopp exclaimed.

"Well, I really like your t-shirt too, man. Did you write and draw on it yourself?"

"Yes… but I really like yours. You want to trade?" he asked.

"You're serious, aren't you?"

"Yes, do you want to trade now?" I could tell he really meant it, so I agreed to the trade. Bebopp began pulling his shirt off. I was a bit embarrassed to take my shirt off in public, but this was a really important moment for me. I was getting blessed by my new friend, in turn, blessing him— no greater feeling in the world than the gift of giving and receiving. I was excited and proud to wear a shirt created by a street-artist. Especially created by this sweet guy.

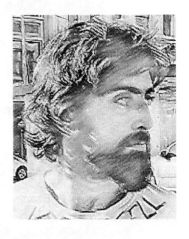

It wasn't until later, while I was at home going through the photos I'd taken, that I paid attention to what was written on his clothing. I found myself zooming in on the photos to get a better look. What I discovered was profound. It was Love.

An example of what I found in Bebopp's heart (love) had been scrolled intentionally upon his own clothing along with these words; Hope, Faith,

Truth (and more). He even wrote his favorite verse from the bible on his sweatpants.

Many of us complain, with bitterness and resentment, about 'those' bums and low-life's camped around town. Or about that disgraceful eye-sore of a pathetic homeless camp down the block. I know, I used to. We fume, we fuss, and we cuss. Pridefully and arrogantly, many of us swear that God will have his way with these detestables... his judgment and his wrath soon to pour out upon these worthless addicts and thieves!

Yet instead, Love sends a message to all, through an unlikely character like Bebopp, who wrote on his clothing, John 3:17: *"For, God [Love] did not send his Son into the world to 'judge' {nor condemn} the world guilty, but to save the world through him [through love and sacrifice]."*

I've spent most of my life judging others. I know now that I was truly not listening to the message of Love. I am now encouraged and challenged to NOT continue to judge and tarnish our world with the 'disability' to share compassion, love, and hope with others.

Maybe, just maybe, those so-called bums and low-lifes, Dirty Kids, Travelers, Homebums, AND those eyesores of a pathetic homeless camp (where a lonely heart calls home), are simply there for us to love uncondi-tionally (maybe even extravagantly) without judgment, testing our hearts, if you will.

The Gift of Mikey & the Dollar Ice Cream

It was a Monday evening in 2016; depression and my tendency to isolate had stalked me all weekend. I was feeling lonely. Thoughts were at war in my mind; the lie that no one cares battled against a positive perspective warning me, *'those thoughts were simply not true.'* The desire for some kind of comfort called to me above the noise. I wanted (even feeling the need) to enjoy *something*. My mom's cooking is the best comfort food in the whole world! All my friends who've eaten her food will attest to that. But she's 65 miles away. I only had a dollar in my wallet. I wondered what I could spend that dollar on that might be a real treat and help to brighten my mood.

Then a thought curiously popped into my head, "McDonald's soft serve vanilla ice cream cones are on sale for a buck." My mind began to race. I can certainly walk the 20 blocks straight down Burnside Street to get one. I could use the exercise as well. "I *love* McDonalds's soft-serve cones. Next to mom's cooking, they are one of my favorite comfort foods!"

Grabbing a lightweight jacket, I put on my shoes and headed out the door. I don't remember much about that walk on the sidewalk of West Burnside because of what happened next.

The pangs of loneliness were still with me when I reached the steps of McDonald's. Then something very bizarre jolted me back to the present, out of my pain and thoughts of despair, and into a state of wonder. I noticed a young man, disheveled and spun out of his gourd, standing at the top of the steps next to the door. When I reached the top of the steps, he grabbed the door handle opening the door for me. What happened next still astounds me and warms my heart to this very day. He shoved a dollar bill into the palm of my hand and with slurred speech, said, *"This is for your vanilla ice cream cone."*

I was shocked and overwhelmed. How did he know?!! Bewildered, I said, "Thank you." Then I went to the counter and placed my order. I even looked at the dollar bill with amazement as I handed it to the cashier. Then with that gift of an ice cream in my hand, I turned to find the young man sitting at a nearby table. He asked me to join him. There was something much more than comfort food happening here.

Mikey was his name. He wore cutoffs, a t-shirt and old tennis shoes. Large brown spots covered his legs, along with a few scabs. I knew his situation all too well, especially after spending more than three months in an inpatient drug and alcohol treatment center called Awakenings By The Sea, in Seaside, Oregon, just three years before. There, I witnessed young people admitted for heroin addiction at an alarming rate. I learned to love all those kids dearly during that stay. As a result, I naturally steer my thoughts away from judgment when I see the telltale symptoms of heroin use. Here was a precious young man that had given me a simple yet profound gift and shared his time with a lonely old guy. How could I ever judge him?!

Conversation with Mikey was somewhat challenging, but I learned more about his big heart in spite of that. Mikey is a gift; his generosity touched me deeply. I already loved this young man. These are the unexpected moments that sometimes lead me from the sidewalks into the hearts of the most unlikely street characters.

May Love bless Mikey in ways we simple humans may never understand. This old guy is very grateful for Mikey and his giving heart. That heart of his changed my whole world that lonely, embittered evening. I really didn't want to return home. I wanted to stay and enjoy more of the love I discover nearly every day in the hearts of the misjudged and misunderstood sidewalk dwellers.

"Downtown Josh"

Josh's greeting and smile on a street corner in downtown Portland were all I needed to stop and chat for a while. Josh tells me, "If people just knew my story, who I am, how I just want to make people smile and have a better day, maybe they would look at me differently. Sitting here on this corner, I don't want anyone to feel sorry for me, but I'm judged every day by people passing by looking at me as though I'm a lowlife. People say I should just get a job. It will solve all my problems." Josh explained all this to me; he and I both knew that it was not the answer. Josh deals with a life-threatening illness, the loss of his family, and the trauma often experienced by Veterans of war. He was just over 30 years old when I first met him.

Josh has the saddest but most beautiful eyes. He wanted me to know his story, and he hoped that someone would really care, and simply love him and the others on the streets, unconditionally rather than judge him. Josh's sharing of his heart brought tears to my eyes. I started to sob, apologizing to him. Josh stood up and hugged me. He knew beyond a shadow of a doubt that I cared and loved him unconditionally. And in turn, he loved me.

This was one of the most poignant experiences I'd experienced up to this point with the street community. As a result, I now weep for the forgotten and avoided smiles and the lost dreams. I weep for the loss of our world, treasuring simple, intimate moments like this one with Josh. Instead, strife and selfishness often rob us of the beauty of simply loving one another.

I weep for the love-deserted landscape of our communities.... communities lost in the distraction of our wanna-be, mask-covered world, and our often stone-cold hearts. I weep for Downtown Josh, but somehow, my tears turn to joy as I remember Josh's eyes, his smile, his embrace, and how he longed to make me smile. And that he was one of the first in the street community who took *my* tears. Josh lovingly and compassionately treasured each one.

The Love Rap

It was the summer of 2016. Walking along Third [Street], on my way home from a doctor's appointment, I noticed Sidewalk sitting with a group of kids on a street corner up ahead of me. I always check in with her, so I walked over to the group. They sat quietly on the sidewalk, chatting and smiling away. I noticed a few new faces. I made it a goal to introduce myself to newcomers, so I thought I could introduce myself before I headed home.

"Chuck ...come sit," Sidewalk called out. She always invites me into her circles; she and I are family. Sidewalk gave me a warm hug as I sat down between her and a young man with brown shoulder-length hair. He was a good-looking kid, maybe 19 years old. He quietly began rapping a song, all the while looking at me. I listened to his song, but it was when our eyes locked that I began to listen more intently. It seemed he was making the song up on the spot as many rap artists do. The words of the song were about someone who cared about others. It was a feel-good rap. After he finished, I said, "Dude! That was awesome! Did you just make that up?!"

"Yes," was his sheepish reply. He almost seemed embarrassed.

"That was talent, man! Do you do that a lot?"

Still a bit shy and reserved, he said, "I've never done it before. Did you really like it?"

"Absolutely!" I assured him. "But, do you mean you made that up right now?" He replied with a 'yes.'

"To make that up off the top of your head is a lot of talent, man! Why did you decide to do that right now?"

"I did it for you," he said, looking up into my eyes.

"Dude! What? Why would you do that for me?" I asked, yet, something deep inside me knew it was Love and tears began to well up in my eyes.

"Because you're a good guy, that's why I did it for you. I know you really care about us." He smiled at me, and I'm sure he noticed the tear rolling down my cheek. He then lovingly gave me a strong hug... and Love's arms wrapped around the two of us. Sidewalk looked on with a proud, knowing smile. Due to opening my mind and my heart to the sidewalks of my world, Love walked through the door, offering me "treasures" beautifully filled with hope and love.

The Warmth of an Unwanted Path

It had only been about three weeks since I moved from the shelter program in Transition Projects Clark Center, into my apartment. Money was a bit tight then. Times like these, when accessing local resources for meals, food boxes, and clothing; are an essential part of everyday life.

Standing in line one morning at the 10 am snack time in the downtown Portland Rescue Mission, I ran into James, one of my beloved street buddies. As is always the case, he gave me a big hug. Sitting together at the cafeteria-style folding tables and chairs in that old dank building, just off Burnside, we each scarfed down hot breakfast sandwiches made of egg, bacon, and pepper jack cheese on sourdough bread. That meal was topped off by a pretty darn good donut and a cup of coffee. All the while, my sweet street buddy shared with everyone around us the depth of God's love for them. I thoroughly enjoyed James's genuine heart for others. I found myself feeling proud of our friendship and that I got to sit with him at the table. James is one of my street buddies with autism.

"James," I said as I got up to leave. "It is so good to see you, man. I love and care about you. You know that, right?"

James smiled while he stood, turning towards me with arms open wide. "I know you do, Chuck. And I love you too."

Touched deeply by the warmth of James' infectious smile and gentle heart, as well as that delicious breakfast snack, I began looking for a garbage can as I left, heading toward Couch Street. That's when I heard the voice of a woman screaming and yelling from down the street. I wasn't sure what all the yelling was about, and not wanting to wreck my good mood or have my PTSD kick in, I hoped to avoid the situation altogether.

As I turned to walk west on Couch, I tried distracting myself from the chaos up ahead by checking my phone for messages and continuing to look for a garbage can. The fact that the yelling was increasing in volume let me know I was getting much closer to the situation. I hoped the problem would resolve itself or would diffuse. Despite not wanting to, I continued to walk toward it.

Moments later, I looked up from my phone. Just up ahead on the corner, an older woman sat on the stoop of a local business. She looked disheveled, her face gaunt, her body thin and frail. She wore a sad expression on her face. She had an even sadder look in her eyes. She wore a multicolored scarf fashioned somewhat like a turban around her head. The clothing she wore certainly was not adequate for our crisp fall weather.

At this point, I realized a young woman with dark hair and a hard streetwise appearance stood next to the old woman. She was the person responsible for all the screaming and yelling. I wasn't sure if the younger woman was yelling at her older companion. As I drew nearer, it was apparent that the old woman was distraught and in need of help.

The route I needed to take to my destination would pass right by the two women unless I turned around and went around the block. I found myself almost instinctively walking across the street directly toward them. As I drew nearer, the younger woman decreased the frequency of her outbursts; she was now quieting down a bit. I began to wonder if the woman was yelling at me. But without hesitation, I continued on my path towards them.

Now within ten feet of the two, the old woman sitting on the step looked up at me, softly pleading, "Could you help me up?"

I wanted to continue walking past them and was mindful that I was a tad fearful of the situation. But when someone asks me for help, well then, I've got to approach that. No matter how I feel in these situations, I find myself on autopilot.

I stopped in front of them without saying a word, set my garbage down on the steps on the right of the old woman, moved around to her left side, and knelt next to her. I softly said, "Now we are going to do this together. I'm going to put my arm up under your arm like this." With that said, I began to show her what I was planning to do to help her stand. I continued to verbally walk her through the process by outlining exactly what we were going to do and that we were going to do it together. This comes very naturally to me from my years of training and experience working in hospitals and medical clinics.

"I'm going to put my arm up under your arm like this. Then I will count one, two, three." Now this haggard and precious old woman, with our face's inches apart, and an expression of uncertainty and pain, looked directly into my eyes and I into hers. Our eyes locked, as I confidently said, "One" ...and she counted with me not letting go of our gaze nor me, "two" ... then... "three!" As we very slowly rose together, her shaking and me using all the strength I could muster in my legs to bear her weight, I saw gratefulness and appreciation in her eyes. Regardless of the smell of alcohol on her breath, or her current life situation, none of that mattered to me. What mattered at that moment was this precious old woman and her knowing someone was there for her, who cared and accepted her just how she is.

It was at this point I realized her young friend had been quiet the whole time. Now with the situation diffused, I had a moment to offer her my attention discovering she was an endearing character for certain. I noticed scars across her face and makeup smeared here and there. She simply looked like a real roughneck of sorts. With a husky voice, after I told them to take really good care of themselves, the young woman gave me a warm smile and said, "Thank you."

This was another one of those amazing sidewalk moments where love has no bounds. I bid them both a warm goodbye and made sure the older one would be able to walk okay. I asked her friend to stay with her to the next destination.

Appearances are so deceiving. The tone or loud sound of a person's voice can also be deceiving. I learned that what I thought was anger was mostly the frustration of the younger woman not understanding the needs of her older friend. There had simply been a miscommunication between the two. I witnessed these two women coming to that conclusion and apologizing to one another. I suppose I filled a vacuum or hole, where living on the streets and with addictions can cause hopelessness, frustration, miscommunications, and ultimately anger. I suppose the hole was replaced by an old guy's gentle and willing heart to help.

All that mattered for me was that moment where I got to honor, respect, and help two individuals in distress on the sidewalk of a downtown street corner where an unplanned destination and unwanted path led me to love.

The Teen, HIV & Me

I remember a night walking to 7 Eleven on Fourth [Street], just planning to get a soda. This is a location on Fourth where I often find Jeff, Litebulb, Swift, and Jesus, among a few others. I chatted briefly with a couple of my friends before entering the store to get my soda. But, before I could, a tall young man whom I did not know walked up to me. I smiled at him and said, "hello." He seemed to hesitate for a moment, then timidly, and with a bit of difficulty finding the words, said, "Can I ask you a question?"

"Sure," I replied with a big smile. "But I'm not sure I'll have an answer."

In response, his words came out slowly, almost with a stutter. Quietly he asked, "What… what do you think of … of people with HIV?"

I was astounded and wondered how long he had waited to ask someone older this difficult question. I was the age his grandfather might be. But here I was, all too familiar with what life is like living with HIV; the challenges, heartbreaks, but most of all, the stigma. Can you imagine my response? He, not knowing me, had just asked this question of someone he'd never met, who has lived with HIV for over half of his life.

"Are you kidding me?" I asked him, knowing that he might think my delight was quite odd. "Do you know who you're asking?" I chuckled, then with understanding and compassion said, "I've lived with HIV for 31 years. I'm healthy, strong, and have never had an HIV-related illness."

This began a conversation where I learned that he was 19 years old, having been infected when he was 15 or 16. He needed someone to talk to. Someone that understood what he was going through and could walk alongside him at that moment. Love brought this young man and me together that night. I hope that he remembers my story. And that he remembers how Love gave him the perfect person to trust and confide in, and where courage and hope appeared out of the blue, profoundly and lovingly calling to him.

Kobin, Rush & the Freezing Cold Night

It was late on a bitterly cold winter night when I came across Rush and his buddy as I walked past a recessed entranceway to a coffee shop just half a block from my apartment. I was in a hurry to get home, desperately needing to get warm and settle in for the night. I hadn't the slightest inkling that I'd come across a street buddy or other unsheltered individuals.

Hearing a familiar voice surprised me as I quickly strode down the sidewalk. An almost inaudible "Hey Chuck" came from the darkness to my left. It was then that I saw the familiar wheelchair and Rush wearing only a t-shirt, jeans, and tennis shoes. He was bent over with his chest in his lap and arms tucked inside his t-shirt in a failing attempt to keep warm. He shivered uncontrollably. Rush had a friend with him, sitting next to his wheelchair, with only a piece of cardboard between him and the ice-cold pavement. There was an empty look of sadness on their faces. "Do you have a blanket I can use just for the night?" Rush asked, his jaw quivering from the cold.

This soft heart of mine wanted desperately to take the two indoors, but it was a Saturday night, the weekend security guard was at his station in the lobby of my apartment building. The homeless are not allowed to enter the building. That thought created anxiety and heartbreak within me. I felt angry over the rampant social injustice in our society, meant to *'keep the riff-raff out.'* That 'riff-raff mentality' was soon becoming my new pet peeve.

Then something a homeless woman once said to me echoed through my mind, *"Why don't people take us in off the streets during this freezing weather?"* With that reminder, there was no way in hell I was going to let these two be alone out in the cold. "If I can't bring them into my apartment," I thought to myself, "then I will stay out in that cold with them all night if I must, to help keep them warm."

I didn't have to look long at the two or ponder the situation much, for compassion and love to rise within me. The tragic thing is, Rush is an amputee, having lost his legs below the knee to frostbite the previous winter. Not more than nine months before, Rush had fallen asleep somewhere downtown. Due to physical exhaustion, he had failed to completely cover his hands and lower legs before falling asleep, leaving them exposed. Not only that but a few of his fingers had also been amputated, and more of them were showing signs of deterioration. They were likely in need of amputation as well. "Damn it, guys!" I exclaimed. "I want to take you to my place, but the building management and security will stop me if I do. They've already warned me several times. I'll be right back, okay?"

It took only two minutes to make it into the apartment building and up the elevator to my room. Quickly grabbing my comforter off the bed (it had become one of my favorites), another blanket, and a few snacks, I was back out the door in less than a minute. It wasn't much, but it was much better than nothing out in the cold. I'm certain that the security guard wondered what the hell I was doing carrying a big comforter out the front door at that time of night.

A minute later, I was back at that dark entranceway with Rush and his buddy. I handed Rush the comforter. He climbed out of his wheelchair without any help from us, immediately curling up in the corner on a piece of cardboard and wrapping the comforter tightly around him. His wheelchair now sat idly by. Then, handing his buddy the blanket, I introduced myself, "I'm Chuck." For the sake of anonymity, I will call Rush's friend "Kobin."

Kobin reached out with his left hand to shake mine, keeping his right hand behind his back. We chatted while Rush fell asleep. I soon learned that Kobin was a sweet young man. He had long dark hair, a short beard, a colorful knit cap atop his head, and gentle eyes. I also found that he is a very bright and intuitive man. I struggled a bit working to keep up with his high level of intelligence but found our conversation very stimulating. I do not remember what the topic was, but there were tones of existentialism, spirituality, and the meaning of Life.

What I DO remember is that he kept his right arm behind his back during our entire conversation. I wondered about this a bit and eventually found myself asking him about it. "I notice you keep your arm behind your back."

"Well, yes," was Kobin's hesitant and soft reply, his eyes looking down at the blanket covering his lap. "My hand gets cold," he simply stated.

Why in the world I approached the situation, I do not know. I only knew it felt right. I found myself asking Kobin if I could warm his hand up for him. This was awkward, even for me, but at that moment, it was almost like an out-of-body experience, watching this whole thing play out between two men on a cold night, with little shelter from the elements. My hands outstretched, ready and willing, compassion swept through my entire being and his eyes locked onto mine. With a look of amazement (maybe just my perspective), he slowly and willingly pulled his hand from behind him, placing it in mine.

I wrapped both of my hands around his as if it were the most natural thing in the world. Kobin's hand was VERY cold; he wasn't making that up! And it was also very stiff; his fingers curled inward as if locked into place by some dark force. Kobin's hand was withered, yet NO force of darkness was going to keep me from loving this young man through the warming of his hand in mine.

As I gently massaged Kobin's hand, we continued to chat. I blew my warm breath over his hand as well. I asked him questions about the circulation in his hand and to what extent he was able to use it. His answers came a bit slowly at first, then more readily as he began getting comfortable with my care and concern for him.

"I play the violin a few blocks from here some evenings," Kobin said in reply to my query of how well he could use his hand.

"You're a busker?" I added with delight. "I'll bet you're pretty good!"

"I think I am," he said with a smile.

"I would love to hear you play sometime."

"I would love that," he said, then described the location of his busking spot.

After a good ten minutes, Kobin said his hand was feeling better. He rested both of his hands in his lap, no longer hiding the one behind his back. I stayed with Rush and Kobin for what seemed like hours.

Maybe we didn't get much warmer in that entryway on Third that cold night. But there was a warmth from companionship, a beautiful moment that transformed my heart's capacity to love into new depths of caring for others, and far more different and beautiful than anything I'd ever known.

Chapter Eight

Lamp Lights and the Hearts of Street Heroes

One late fall afternoon, as the temperature dropped sharply nearing dusk, I invited a few street buddies up to my room for a reprieve from the downtown sidewalks. Freddy and his girl, Sidewalk, came upstairs with me first, and my buddy Zack arrived shortly thereafter, along with another street-buddy, Nico. I brought them up as well. Zack had a box of donuts to share and hoped Nico could come along. I was grateful for my friends and to have another break from the aloneness and the drone of a persistent depressive disorder. It is important to mention that Nico and Freddy did not really know each other. And as is Freddy's nature, he is usually leery of someone he does not yet know.

Almost immediately after we entered my apartment, the bathroom became the central focus. It's a rare moment that the kids get to use one where they can clean up and feel more like a normal person.

Unexpectedly, in the midst of taking turns in the bathroom, Freddy's 'protective disorder' (as I endearingly call it) kicked in. Suddenly we all heard him bark loudly at Nico. "Do not disrespect my girl!"

Without going into detail, a brief verbal altercation exploded into a physical one. The two ended up wrestling almost violently on the kitchen floor within moments, and it took only that long for me to realize my PTSD was kicking in. Regardless, I wanted my buddies to take it outside, on their own turf.

I pleaded with them, "Come on, guys. Please don't do this here. I don't want the neighbors to complain and get you guys kicked out and banned from the building. Freddy ... Nico ...please ... Do this for me."

My attempts to diffuse the situation fell on deaf ears. About a minute into their wrestling match, my PTSD and anxiety were too much for me. I needed to get out of there and take care of myself. I was certain the neighbors could hear the commotion, which added to my anxiety. I was especially concerned about disturbing my sweet friend, Sheri, next door. These guys are young strapping dudes with solid muscles and creating quite a ruckus! Neither was willing to give an inch or to give in to the other. "Guys, I gotta go ..." I blurted out. "My PTSD is really bad. I'll be back."

I then looked to Sidewalk and Zack, asking them to keep an eye on things. Zack has no problem taking care of himself. I knew he would watch over the situation responsibly. Sidewalk was beside herself, wanting Freddy to stop but knowing he was not going to back down.

I turned to leave, realizing that I'd have to step over the top of Nico and Freddy during their embittered battle. This in itself was disturbing to me. I was not so much in distress over the PTSD kicking in or that this was taking place in my home; I was also concerned about my two friends. Concerned that either one might be hurt badly, that the neighbors would be disturbed and call the cops, but mostly concerned that 'hate' would be a result of a battle between two young men, who this old guy has learned to love... dearly.

On the elevator to the first floor I went, exiting the building quickly, uncertain of where I should go. It was darker out now and getting colder. In my urgency to leave my apartment, I didn't stop to dress warmer. But I was now feeling better. I was down on the sidewalk; the place where I have, as of late, felt safe, cared for and loved by the street kids.

I walked towards Waterfront Park, which was only three blocks away, thinking a walk would help to calm me down and hopefully give the wrestling match time to diffuse. I thought once I felt better, I could safely return to my apartment and my friends.

The beautiful soft light created by the lamp posts along the river's waterfront walkways, the glistening of the city lights reflected by the waters, and the colorful lights of the Hawthorne Bridge just to the south, gave no light to the darkness within me as I walked. I was alone and nothing about the evening meant anything to me. I simply wanted my friends to be unharmed and safe. I silently asked Love to be with them.

As I walked south along the promenade, passing lamp post after lamp post, not one of them helped shine a light on the darkness within me. Walking at a slow pace for about ten minutes, I reached the Morrison Bridge, still completely distraught, considering whether I should head home to check on things. But anxiety gripped me each time I approached that thought. I paused for nearly an hour under the bridge, standing next to a pillar, feeling very alone and very anxious.

It wasn't long before I realized it was getting even colder. I needed to start moving to warm myself. I continued south toward the Hawthorne Bridge, where the promenade ends at a turnaround and where the grassy slopes and path along the Willamette River led to the South Waterfront area of downtown. This would normally be a beautiful walk with the view of Mt. Hood and the Willamette to the east; the water sparkling, reflecting light from the bridge and city lights in the evenings. Lamp posts amidst the trees lined the walkway on the right. The tall buildings were aglow with lights towering above the trees. The landscape near Salmon Street Fountain and the promenade turnaround is beautiful, with a palm tree or two among the other tropical plants and colorful flowers.

My walk continued on to where the promenade and the grassy slope meet. Here, it is about a thirty-foot drop from the promenade railing straight down to the water. I decided to walk to where the railing ended and the grass began. I took the four concrete steps down to the pathway with a little apprehension. Here, behind the railing, I found myself under some trees looking out across the river. But I also found it to be much darker than I expected.

Stepping onto the grass, I could barely make out the slope that went down to the river's edge. It was steep. Boulders monopolized the area, making a trek down to the water after nightfall very dangerous indeed. Deciding that venturing down to the water was not a good idea, I turned back to the pathway where, to my surprise, I discovered a park bench nestled under a tree in the dark. The thought of a park bench here by the water's edge under the trees prompted the thought that this could be a safe place where I might refocus and calm myself.

I knew I wouldn't be any warmer if I sat again, but I hoped the calming of my nerves in a somewhat secluded spot would help me to feel safe. Or so I thought... until moments later. Standing next to the bench, I was startled back into the depths of anxiety and fear as I heard a mysterious voice piercing the silence, crystal clear, and coming directly from the darkness behind me.

"Revolver or pistol?" were the simple yet frightening words spoken from out of the darkness.

Instantly, I froze. Still in somewhat of a state of trauma, my first thought was, "This person is going to kill me. They want me to choose the weapon? Holy crap! What do I do now?"

Afraid to move, I quickly, yet nervously, answered with a tone of despair, "I would prefer neither."

"What are you doing down here?" The voice loomed from out of the darkness.

I turned to face that voice before I answered. In the darkness, I could barely see the outline of a tall man with a muscular build just 15 feet away. He stood against the wall of the promenade's foundation where it met the river's edge. "Well," I spoke with sadness to the stranger in the dark. "I had no place to go ... so I came for a walk and ended up here."

"Were you coming down here to harm yourself?" the man asked.

"Oh, NO!" I replied. "I just needed a safe place to be for a while. I live just a few blocks away but had to leave my apartment because there was a fight. I have PTSD."

The man then walked a few steps towards me. Still not close enough that I could make out his features, he stopped and said, "I know all about PTSD. I just got home from Iraq."

At those words, my fear melted into compassion. "Are you homeless?" I asked.

"Yes," was the man's solemn reply.

"Why are *you* down here by the river?" I was now quizzing him. "Were you thinking of harming yourself? Is that why you asked me that question?"

"Well, no," he said. He paused for a moment, then added, "I don't really know anyone yet, and it feels safer here down by the river than in downtown. At least for now. And, it's just that people do come down to the river or bridges to end their lives. I just wanted to make sure you were okay. That you weren't one of them."

I was astounded, "Dude! You were worried about me? You're homeless and have no one, and you're worried about some old guy you don't even know? I don't know what to say... But, thank you, man. It really means a lot."

"My name is Big Red," he said, stepping from out of the darkness into the soft glow of the city lights.

I shook Big Red's hand, honored that he would take time for an old guy like me. Big Red was a handsome young man with red hair and a short beard. To my surprise and joy, he began sharing his faith with me. It was about Jesus and love. He shared about his military experience and the current struggle of recently coming from that environment back into the civilian world, along with the uncertainty of what life would look like for him now.

I don't remember the exact conversation, but I do remember that it was poignant, bittersweet, even beautiful. Big Red revealed himself to be trustworthy, encouraging, and a protector. Something I truly needed that evening. He cared about me and wanted to make sure I was okay and that I knew Jesus was with me. "I don't live my life like I think God might want me to," he said, looking down at the ground. "But I want people to know that God really cares about them."

"Thank you, Big Red. I honestly believe that and really needed that reminder at this very moment." I asked Big Red if he would come with me back to my apartment to make sure it was safe. He declined, and I saw he shared an anxiety that was all too familiar.

Then he offered me this insight, "Man, I want you to be safe, and I want to feel safe as well. Right now, being down here by the river is my safe place. I hope you don't mind."

"I get it, Big Red. Boy, do I get it," I said with a smile.

As I was thanking him for chatting with me and helping me out of my distress, we walked up to the promenade and noticed a young woman walking toward us with some apprehension. Simultaneously we agreed that she did not feel safe there with two unknown men in the dark up ahead. We walked to another area so she would feel safer as she passed by. We said a gentle "hello" to her in hopes she might know we understood the feeling of being unsafe. Then we watched out for her from our vantage point while she navigated the dark path crossing the grassy slope along the Willamette River down to the South Waterfront.

I was now beginning to see the beauty of everything around me. The river, city lights, and trees are all very precious to me, along with my new buddy, Big Red. I was grateful for his thoughtful and encouraging words, reminding me that I'm not alone. How could I doubt that now? In my mind, Big Red was sent to look out for me that dark evening, and even in the darkness that lurked within me.

I got a hug from Big Red before walking under the off-ramps of the Hawthorne Bridge, towards Naito Parkway at the edge of Waterfront Park. I was beginning to feel safe but still not wanting to be alone as I again considered returning to my apartment.

I walked for less than three minutes when I heard an all too familiar voice call out, "Chu-uck!" It was my street-buddy Jeff. Even though Chuck is just one syllable, Jeff says it with a happy-go-lucky tone and two syllables. I was relieved. Here was someone I knew. 'I might not be alone after all,' I thought to myself.

"Jeff! Dude! I'm so glad to see you, man!" I shouted with relief.

"What are you doing out here, Chuck?" Jeff asked with concern.

"I had to leave my apartment cause Freddy and Nico got into a fight, and my PTSD kicked in,"

"Wha-at?!" Came Jeff's sing-songy drawn-out reply. "Freddy and Nico? Shit man! What happened?" he asked.

I explained to Jeff that I really didn't know what had happened. I then asked if he could maybe go back to my apartment with me to make sure everything was ok.

"I can't right now," Jeff replied. "But Hippie [Jesus] is right over there." Jeff pointed under the bridge. "I gotta take off. But you can see if he wants to hang out?"

"Sure," I replied back to Jeff. "Where is he?"

Jeff called out towards the underbelly of the Hawthorne Bridge. I assumed in the direction of Jesus. He then led me over to where Jesus was gathering up his belongings and backpack.

"What's up, Jesus?" I asked.

"Oh, nuthin," Jesus replied with that endearing drawl he always speaks with. "What're you up to?"

"Just tryin' to chill after a fight that broke out in my apartment earlier," I explained to him.

"Wha-ut?!" was Jesus' reply. Jesus and Jeff are like two peas in a pod. Jeff said a quick 'goodbye' and was off.

I looked at Jesus, "You mind if I hang out for a while?"

"Not at all," was Jesus' happy reply. "I just gotta go charge my phone. Come with me." He got no argument from me. I was feeling much safer now that I had him with me. We walked to a nearby parking structure, sharing a bit of small talk along the way. Jesus led me to a corner where there were electrical outlets near an elevator. He plugged in his charger and sat on the sidewalk. I joined him, sitting next to a parking ticket machine.

Jesus pulled a few items out of his backpack and began to whittle. He is very good at getting creative as he works on projects without having traditional tools. I never really know what he's making, but I enjoy watching him figure out the best way to accomplish a task with very little to work with. Jesus takes his time and stays patiently focused. The conversation was refreshing. Jesus continued to whittle, and I began to relax.

"I'm a woodcarver," I told Jesus. "It's fun watching you work. It's helping me to relax being here." Jesus smiled and continued his work. About 15 minutes later, I asked Jesus how he felt about walking with me to my apartment.

"Sure," Jesus said without hesitating. I knew he liked getting a reprieve from being on the streets now and then.

"You can finish charging your phone at my place if you like," I offered him.

"Okay," Jesus said, shrugging his shoulders. We picked up his things, and I helped him carry some of his load as he, in turn, was helping me to carry mine. We headed north on Third. The walk to my place was maybe ten blocks. I was grateful to walk with my friend and noticed a huge change in my mood, which took my mind off the cold chill of the night. My load was lighter now. We talked, passing shoppers and storefronts on our journey. The city was looking much brighter to me with peace filling me.

The beauty about the walk home with Jesus was reflected in the outcome I discovered from those battered buddies of mine on Third, when Jesus and I neared my apartment building. Nico was the first voice I heard shouting from up the street. "Chuck! You won't believe what happened!" Nico looked a bit worse for wear but was excited about something and happier than I'd ever seen him.

"We worked it out!" Nico exclaimed. "Everything's okay; Freddy and I are friends now." He was excited to share this with me, which was not what

I expected to hear at all when I returned. "We're both good!" Nico added. "What?! Are you serious?!" I shouted back. Nico came closer, giving me a hug.

Almost with disbelief but with an excitement of my own welling up within me, I said, "This is so awesome, Nico! I'm really proud of you guys. Do you know where Freddy is?"

"Just up the street in his spot. Go see him; he really wants to see you."

"I'm heading there now. I really love you, Nico,"

"See, you had nothing to worry about," Jesus announced with a smile.

"I can't believe this, Jesus," I said with a tone reflecting a hint of disbelief. "Let's head to my place and check in on Freddy first." I was already feeling much better when, within a couple of minutes, we came across Freddy and Side-walk in their usual spot on Third.

"Chuck!" Freddy called out when he saw me. "Nico and I are friends now. I'm sorry we got into it at your place. Everything is okay, and Zack stayed behind to wait for you."

"Freddy, it's no problem as long as you and Nico are okay. And especially since you worked it out. That's all that matters to me. I'm really proud of you guys and love you both!"

"I know Chuck. We love you too. Thanks for caring about us," Freddy said as he hugged me. Then Jesus and I continued on to my apartment, which was just around the corner.

Needless to say, Zack was still patiently sitting by the window as Jesus and I walked through the door. "Dude!" I cried out, grateful that he was still there, keeping an eye on things and making sure that I'd be okay. I told Zack he could hang out as long as he liked that evening. Jesus hung out for a while as well. And soon, Jeff came to join us. I can't help but care about these kids. Love has placed each of them deep in my heart. For me, they are easy to love.

The typical definition of a superhero is a benevolent fictional character with superhuman powers. For me, a superhero is someone with the

superhuman power to not judge; he forgives, respects, and honors others. A superhero is a person, no matter how they may appear, who walks alongside and encourages others in times of distress, especially when they, themselves, are in need or in some type of their own distress. And a superhero is a heart that looks forward to sharing their struggles and joys with those that love them. The street buddies of mine may sound like fictional characters, yet they are real, looking after an old guy like me with profoundly beautiful hearts.

Big Red, Jeff, Jesus, Nico, Freddy, and Zack were my downtown superheroes that evening. A motley crew of misfits, one by one, walking

alongside, encouraging, and sharing life with me. It was an evening where I saw love bloom from the midst of the darkness. This old guy's joy, certainly complete.

Reflecting on how the evening began, with so much darkness and the feelings of emptiness, I realize during this writing that my escape to safety as I walked along the Waterfront was shrouded by the darkness within me. The lamp posts along the promenade could not penetrate that darkness and did little to shed light on a path to safety for me. That walk was lit by something far more valuable and eternal than man-made lamp posts. It was the light of each of the unexpected encounters and hearts of the outcasts (my downtown superheroes) that lit the way and brought me safely home.

Big Red told me about Jesus [Love] being with me, Jeff led me to Jesus, Jesus walked home with me, and my faithful buddy Zack waited at home for me to return. Wow! What a profound metaphor for me to remember as I continue on in my life's journey.

When I apologetically spoke with my neighbors the day after the 'wrestling match' and all the commotion in my apartment, yes, they were home, but no, they didn't hear a sound coming from my apartment the night before. It was a quiet, peaceful evening for each of them. And why was this *not* a surprise me? It's just icing on the cake of the *magic* called *Love*.

This "magic" took me further into readily meeting anyone out on the streets. They were not only welcoming me into their hearts and lives, but I also began to welcome them into mine. This brought me deeper into a world of outcasts that would teach me through their insights and friendships that steering away from judgment is an avenue into better understanding others. And, simply listening to their stories and hearts would help me grasp life's true meaning.

Daily, beautiful "When Sidewalks Smile" moments continue to not only warm this old guy's heart but to soften it as well, convincing me that this world could use this book which shares real-life loving experiences to not only distract us from the deteriorating state of our planet but to help us refocus and rekindle a fire of passion in our world, our hearts, and help us heal our plant.

Chapter Nine

"The Cosmic Tones of Home~Free Nomads"

"Cosmics have the patience of a great tree.
Psychically [they] have been [through] most of what [they]
experience around [them], so are often a good ear for others
because of enduring patience
and perseverance. [They] can often see above the fray of emotional
dramas, transcending the argument or conflict;
offering calm, lucid, objective advice
(from www.another-world.net).
He is liberal, confident, and transcendent."

"Not who I thought I was, and not who I thought I would be."

~Keenan Peters

Keenan & Pizza~dog

This little guy is one of the reasons I love the infamous corner on Third so much. As I walked past the ledge one afternoon in the fall of 2016, I said my usual, "Hey," and nodded to all of my friends, happy to see them as always. That's when I noticed a kid holding a cute little dog, a chihuahua, or a mix, one of my favorite breeds. The young man's face was unfamiliar, so as usual, I introduced myself.

"You don't look familiar; my name's Chuck," I said to him. The young man stood up to shake my hand while still holding that adorable little dog. The kid was short with a sweet smile and a twinkle in his eyes.

"I'm Keenan, and *this*," he happily proclaimed, holding up his pup's little paw, waving it at me, *"is Pizza-dog!"* He made me smile. I chuckled to myself, realizing I was already liking this kid, but maybe at this point, his dog, Pizza, a tad bit more.

Keenan looked younger than his years, though maybe a bit weathered for his age. His hair was brown and naturally woven into some fairly impressive dreadlocks. There was a cherubic look to his features. He wore patched-up coveralls (typical 'Dirty Kid'/'Traveler' attire) that were curiously torn off just below the knees. It appeared that, maybe, it was because he had huge muscular calves for such a little guy. I laugh about it now, only because I know that at the time, I was somewhat envious. We chatted briefly about where he was from. I quickly learned that Keenan is a 'Traveler' from Texas, having just arrived in town.

"You ride the rails?" I asked.

"Yup," Keenan replied, sounding happy. "It's my life. Me and Pizza," he smiled at me.

"A man after my own heart," I said to Keenan. "You love adventure!"

"Yup," he said. He appeared to be in deep thought for a moment as he looked down at that cute little Pizza-dog. There was a lot about Keenan that I did not learn until much later, but in this first meeting, I could tell he hoped that he could trust me.

He looked up at me and said, "I got a problem I need to take care of."

A little concerned, I asked, "What's up? You okay?"

"Yeah, but I need to get indoors for a while to take care of myself." Without asking questions, I knew that I could provide a temporary safe place for him inside.

"Come on up," I offered.

Sounding surprised, he said, "Really?"

"Yeah, man. I don't have much to offer, but it's a safe place. It's the least I can do."

"Cool!" Keenan said with a smile as he gathered up Pizza and a small backpack. He asked a friend to watch his larger backpack rather than haul it around.

Keenan seemed a bit sad in the midst of being a fun-loving character. And what a character he is! He kept me on my toes with his quick wit. Yet, he was dealing with his demons (as we all do at several points in our lives), I think in the best ways he knew how. I let him stay a couple of nights at my place. I wondered how safe he really was on the streets. I would have let him stay longer, but as he mentioned, the kid is full of adventure and loves to travel. Traveling is his safe place. For whatever reason, Keenan enjoys riding the rails around the country. I could only wonder what it was about his story that brought Keenan to make that decision and how long ago that was. Or was it simply his journey in life, his purpose?

Keenan and Pizza went out to the suburbs with me one day on Portland's lite-rail trains to visit one of my closest friends, Doug. We've been friends for 30 years. Pizza played with Doug's two dogs while we all chatted. Doug immediately grew fond of Keenan. He reminded Doug of his younger brother, Larry, who was also short and fun-loving with a quick wit like Keenan. He, too, had that gentle cherubic look about him, and Larry battled many demons in his life as well. Sadly, Larry died many years ago. I, too, knew and loved Larry. Doug was right; Keenan was a lot like Larry in many ways. But mostly, it was the sweet and innocent cherubic appearance that hid a difficult and complicated life. *THAT, I was certain of.*

Before we left, Doug took me aside, asking if Keenan was okay and if he needed anything. I mentioned a few things that would help him out. As is Doug's generous nature, he gave me some cash for Keenan. It warmed my heart that someone else saw something special in Keenan, wanting to make sure, as well, that he would be okay.

A glimpse into Keenan's heart comes from the lyrics of two songs he has posted on a social network. 'Jammin' was the simple word he wrote in one post. These songs are special to Keenan in some way. Songs by *Dark Dark Dark* called *'Heavy Heart'* and *'In Your Dreams.'* The instrumentals and vocals are an interesting upbeat blend of New Orleans jazz, Americana, Eastern European folk, and pop aesthetic influences. The lyrics are haunting and a glimpse into Keenan's world of his tortured heart, the sadness, and the loneliness he often experiences.

Dark Dark Dark

'In Your Dreams'   *https://youtu.be/9oyC5S8QfKE*

'Heavy Heart' on WNYC's Spinning On Air

https://youtu.be/1BLXAEc48og

I didn't understand at the time, but when Keenan stayed at my place, he liked being close. I found it to be one more of his many special qualities. And one that led *this old guy* to wonder if maybe Keenan doesn't like being alone. He would sit or lay on the couch next to me while watching TV. It was like way back in the day, having a kid at home again. Pizza would happily sit on the back of the loveseat across the room or between us (years earlier, my wife and I always wondered if, and hoped, we might have a son one day, we were blessed with two beautiful daughters). I liked having this kid around, and I was getting to experience a whole new side to the father/son relationship.

To this day, when I think about Keenan, he is one of those young men that I would love to have as a son. I told him this on one occasion. "Keenan, if I ever had a son, I would want him to be a lot like you." He smiled and hugged me.

During our chats, I noticed something remarkable about this young man. He has a father's heart. Watching him interact with Pizza and his buddies in a very kind, gentle, and thoughtful manner.

"Keenan," I asked him on one occasion. "Have you ever thought about having kids someday?"

"Yup, I really want to be a dad someday," he said, his heart shining through his words and his smile.

"You're going to be a great father," I assured him. "I can see it in your heart, in how good you are with others and with Pizza. You're even patient with *ME*," I chuckled.

Keenan's smile was his only response. There were no words. Just that sweet smile.

In 2014, Keenan and Pizza had traveled to New Orleans. They were on the streets when Keenan was attacked and beaten by a group of seven men one night. Traumatized by the incident and to Keenan's horror, Pizza ran off into the darkness. The most important thing to Keenan in the world is Pizza-dog and his companionship. But now, battered and bruised, Keenan was feeling *VERY* lost and even more alone than *EVER*. He had lost his precious Pizza-dog, having no hope in somehow, or someday, ever finding him.

The following is a link to a YouTube video of a TV program on Animal Planet that reunites lost pets with their owners. By watching this segment of that program, you will see Keenan's heart and his beautiful, loving relationship and powerful bond with that sweet little dog, just as this old guy has.

"REUNITED! "This Pup Is So Excited To Be Back With His Owner"

https://youtu.be/IZnchIFlw40

The last night he stayed at my apartment was the night after we returned to my place from Doug's. Keenan seemed to be very introspective about something. "I want to make some changes," he said, looking me in the eye while we stood chatting in my kitchen.

"What do you mean?" I asked.

"I think I want to start by cutting off my dreads," Keenan answered.

"*WHAT*?" I asked with surprise and a tone of confusion in my voice. "***Why? Are you sure?***"

"It's time," Keenan said with determination, immediately asking, "Do you have scissors?"

"Well, yes, but ..." I responded hesitantly. "Are you sure you don't want to ...maybe ... think about this overnight?" I asked.

"Nope," Keenan said with his determination intact. And with that, he stood in the kitchen and cut off all of his dreads.

We picked his hair up from the floor together. I didn't want to throw his dreadlocks away. For me, there was some kind of loss attached to them. They had been an important part of who Keenan is. Or maybe (or not) it was a sort of *'rite of passage'* that I'd just been honored to witness.

Regardless, my heart wouldn't let me throw his dreadlocks in the trash. I carefully put them in a plastic Ziplock bag, placing it on the counter in the bathroom. I did not know why, but this kid was really getting to me. It was like watching one of my own kids as they go through the many changes and periods of growth in their lives. The *'father heart'* within me was stirred deeply by my young friend.

For me, the difficult part of this story is how Keenan and I parted ways before he left Portland. We had a miscommunication resulting in me *thoughtlessly* lecturing him on a choice he was making. Maybe I was upset because I loved this little guy too much and was afraid for him, fearing where he was headed in life. I was reminded, at that moment, of Larry, Doug's younger brother. It's like, in my mind, my *'father heart'* wanted to help, but I was misguided by the *'forgetting'* of my own past and my own questionable choices. I was forgetting about how I *desperately needed* others to be patient and understanding towards me at those difficult times in life.

Yet, here with Keenan, I placed my fear of seeing myself and my failures and carelessly projected them onto him. The truth about how I handled that situation came to me a bit too late, but in retrospect, I've learned that nurturing, acceptance, compassion, and understanding are all Keenan really needed that day. He simply wanted to know he was loved unconditionally.

Keenan did not argue with me about my rant. He stayed calm and attempted to reiterate his perspective on the situation, which is Keenan's respectful nature with me. He did seem to be disappointed. Still, to this very day, even as I write this, I regret my careless words.

After that, I've always hoped I'll see Keenan and Pizza-dog again, to have the opportunity to tell Keenan how sorry I am for not having been more understanding and compassionate with him. But mostly, I want to tell him how sorry I am for failing to nurture him, as any parent or adult should, yet, we too often blindly forget, we too, once walked a similar path, having to learn from our own choices and mistakes.

As far as regrets, I've had many in my life. My failure to be more understanding with Keenan is among the *WORST* of all of my regrets. I learned something of great value through my experience with him. Always be kind and gentle and *NEVER* judge anyone or their actions. For, if I am not more caring and understanding towards others, I may not only wound their heart but darken my own in the process. This old guy carries this sweet, fun-loving little guy in my heart every day.

"I love you, Keenan Peters and your precious Pizza-dog, but not as much as I've grown to love you and your tender heart!"

~Poppa Chuck

Connor Peters

Keenan hadn't mentioned his twin brother, Connor, but through the magic of cyberspace, I met their mother, Suzy Bianchi-Barrett. Somehow, I feel I know Connor through my connection with Keenan. But it is through Suzy, their mom, that I now have a peek into Connor's heart and find myself loving him as well.

Suzy received her Reiki Master/Teacher attunement while she was pregnant with Connor (they called him 'Bear' (or Connor-Bear) and Keenan, they called 'Boy,' (an endearing nickname given to their uncle that stuck with him throughout his life). The following was told to me by *Suzy, a beautiful picture she paints...*

"*To say Keenan and Connor are in touch with others' emotions is an understatement. One day, when Connor was not quite two, the dog came in from the backyard, limping. He flopped onto the cement floor. Connor toddled over, wearing nothing but his cloth diaper, the plastic cover, and munching on his pacifier. He squatted down next to the dog's leg, placed both hands on its haunch, and closed his eyes. After a few moments, he sighed, stood up, and toddled away onto the next thing. The dog got up and followed him like he'd never been hurt.*

Like his brother, Keenan knew instinctively when someone or something was hurt. In many ways, I blame myself for their emotional doors being laid wide open. They are degrees beyond your average 'empaths.' Keenan was born first, then Connor one minute later, both born as Reiki Masters.

Connor didn't talk until he was almost three years old. Keenan, on the other hand, started having conversations by age one and rarely left opportunities for anyone to respond. He was like Mortimer Mouse.

They are polar opposites when it comes to expression. Keenan is all about action, determined and tenacious about every task he saddles himself with. He thrives on praise. It was all about immediate gratification.

Connor is the observant one. He watches and will assess, then give you his opinion. He taught himself to read a year before anyone realized he could. He didn't like drawing attention to himself. At first glance, one would assume he was sullen or irritated. It was his expression when he was mulling over whatever situation was tumbling through his mind.

Of the two, Connor was the one to cry more easily. He was very private but never so much as to hide his very sensitive being. Keenan would hide when he cried. More often than not, his emotions would turn angry as if to squash his feelings because they were a sign of 'weakness' in his mind.

One time Connor called me from New York City. He and his girlfriend were arguing, and then she began hitting him, trying to incite a physical fight. Connor walked away, called me, and between sobs told me what had happened. He wanted me to know that he had been badly hurt and no longer wanted to be with his girlfriend. Connor refused to hit back and could not be in a relationship with someone who thought it was ok to hit. I was so proud of him.

I think things went south for them when their father left us. They watched me go from a size 22 to a size 4 in eight months. That first few months, they had witnessed their father and the woman he'd met online take out furniture and things they'd grown up with. At age 9, they learned their father had not only left us for this new woman but had lied to their mother, to them, and their three sisters. Sadly, they lost respect for their father.

At age 10, a legal custody battle placed them with their father. Through that heartbreaking and devastating experience, both boys, being torn away from their mother, now resented their father. Ten months after that, thankfully, I got them back. Once safely home with me, it was a rare occasion that they saw or spoke to their father after that.

Sometimes one or the other of the boys would call him if they wanted something. Almost invariably, the conversation would end in an argument, and then months would go by before they would call him again.

They began to skip school, hanging out with the 'seedier' side of the population and experimenting with drugs. Neither would bathe or brush their teeth. They then began hopping trains and self-medicating. But, usually come back home.

They saw their oldest sister, Rebecca, like a second mom. They adored her daughter, Sammy. There were 11 years between Rebecca, Keenan, and Connor. But only 7 years and 2 days between them and Sammy."

A Darkness the Family could not Fathom

Life took a tailspin into a darkness that any family could not fathom. Tragedy after tragedy rocked the boy's world, eventually ending in the loss of Rebecca and Sammy. They died in a house fire under suspicious circumstances. Fear and anger were at an all-time high for the boys. It was like they had to relive the heartache and brokenness attached to being torn away from their mother. Now their older sister Rebecca (whom they loved dearly, considering her a second mom), along with their precious niece, had been ripped from their hearts as well.

"The emotional toll of all this sent the boys careening. Their alcohol and drug use became a daily need to escape their emotions. They felt guilty that they couldn't protect Sammy and Rebecca. They were angry that they couldn't exact revenge on the people who had hurt their loved ones. Connor, in particular, had trouble even coming home because there were too many memories. Two beautiful souls had been taken and left two damaged souls behind.

Connor is such a gentle person. He and Keenan would hold my hand when we walked anywhere. Even inside the grocery store. They never went through that 'I don't know you in pub-

160

lic' phase that some boys do. And every phone call or sending off after a visit end with, '*I love you, Mom.*'

They'd bring their friends home to meet me. Many of their friends would ask me to cut their hair (I'm not a stylist), but only because they trusted me. Dozens of their friends still call me 'Mom.' According to them, Connor and Keenan adore me."

Suzy Bianchi-Barrett, thank you so much for introducing this old guy to your son, Connor, and sharing a mother's beautiful insights into the hearts of her Dirty Kid sons. YOUR heart has bridged a gap across the sidewalks of cyberspace, connecting the world to a better understanding of what goes on in the hearts and lives of those we often judge and misunderstand. A'Ho and love to you, my friend!

~Poppa Chuck

"*If you've ever been homeless, an addict, or just dealt a bad hand in life, struggling, etc., that shit hits differently when you see someone on the street. Be kind to everyone, everyone has a story, and I swear to God (speaking to her social network friends) if I ever see you talking down or mistreating some-one on the street, you will no longer be a part of my life. Peri-oddddddd!!! Much love.*" ♥

~Sarah Boude (one of the boys adopted moms)

~

On the Mayan calendar, Keenan and Connor's Galactic Birthday falls on a 'Cosmic' tone day, which is the same tone as Bilbo Bagginz.

"**A 'Cosmic' activates by being a disciple of the present moment cultivating their capacities to be wakeful and receptive to each new now; by going beyond the rational mind and letting one-self think with their ancient heart; by being conscious of their**

161

boundlessness, while still living in the moment; by learning to 'ride the spiral,' ascending to higher levels of being; by allowing their cosmic spirit to carry them through the many journeys of trial and triumph this life has to offer; by transcending fears of the future; by transcending regrets of the past; by transcending the limits of linear time and synchronizing with the radial flow of synchronic reality; by recognizing us all to be but evolving children of an ever-unfolding Creation."

(From https://www.13moon.com)

Bilbo Space Bagginz

"I smell bacon frying in the cornfields
where all the clowns gather
and declare when summer starts and
ends on a dime in my pocket,
in my coat of lavish lavender,
flowers in my hair."

What can this old guy say about the heart of a precious young man like Bilbo? Words are not enough to define this young and very wise man. I met Bilbo on a social network, through my friendship with Sidewalk (of course). I immediately fell in love with Bilbo's 'wordsmithing' talents. His work speaks volumes, and his heart tells a story, one of a *Love that encompasses ALL.*

"When the glorious one comes upon the earth, we will then see that his glory is undying. We will then see that we are all one in the same."

~Bilbo Space Bagginz

> ## Ode to Dogs
> ### By Bilbo Space Bagginz
>
> They are always to be your best friend
> To the day that life does surely end
> They love you more than anything
> When you're angry they can feel the sting
> When you're happy they will rejoice with you
> When you're sad they know just what to do
> They are your best friends in life
> No person can match or fit just right
> Always treat them with love and care
> Because dogs can always be right there.

Chatting with Bilbo through Messenger one afternoon, he didn't hold back when it came to answering questions about his life and his heart. When asked if he chose his nickname or if it was his friends who gave it to him, he explains, *"It's actually 'Bilbo Space Bagginz,' but most people call me 'Bilbo' or 'Hobbit.' A couple of kids gave me the name a few years ago. It started with Hobbit or 'Hobbit Daddy,' from 'Daddy Camp' at Bluegrass Regionals. Then ended up being what it is now when we were at the National Rainbow Gathering."*

Bilbo explained to me when asked if he considered himself a Dirty Kid or a Traveler; *"I'm a Traveler. I've been traveling on and off since 2015. Traveling is the only way I feel 'at home' right now. Maybe it'll be like that for my whole life, maybe not. I hope to have a communal farm eventually. I started traveling right after my 19th birthday.*

I've always loved the idea of living in the 60s and traveling. And the way it was back then. Ever since I was a kid, 'Hippies' fascinated me. So, I eventually got the guts to try it. Even with being convinced that the lifestyle of the 'Hippies' was all dead and gone and had been since the 60s and 70s, I decided I wanted that lifestyle because of my hometown and how I was raised.

Truth is, I raised myself most of my childhood. I have ADD/ADHD, extreme anxiety disorder, and major depressive disorder. I think I have some kind of trauma-related issues too. To cope with all of that, I spent most of my time building stuff with Legos, playing outside, and on the computer. My escape into the computer world began after I reached a certain age."

There were moments during the online chat when I needed to take a break and collect myself. Some of Bilbo's childhood reflected that of my own. I am amazed and so proud of this young man for not only surviving but thriving by following his heart to live free and to love others unconditionally.

When asked to tell me about his heart, Bilbo hesitates, *"I don't know how to."* Then he wrote: *"I believe in unconditional love and understanding for everyone. Free hugs! BUT, if a person is an asshole, call them out on it. Do it because you love them. Then, give them a hug when they've corrected it."*

A quote of Bilbo's that intrigues this old guy offers a glimpse into the insights and the freedom that is the heart and soul of Bilbo Space Bagginz: ***"I am the dragon you chase, the change in your pace, the drug that you taste, for, I AM FREE!"***

"I wrote this as part of a poem I posted a long time ago. I made that my introduction on a social network." When complimented on his many talents and wisdom, Bilbo humbly responds with, *"I'm just living and doing things that make sense."*

This brings to mind Bilbo's busking talents. Bilbo tells me, *"Busking is more than a way to earn money."* He adds, *"Busking is spreading ART to people. For me, giving them a new perspective, a new way to want to hear a song. I don't have a good busking instrument right now, I do have a harmonica, but I like to sing when I busk. I enjoy singing; it makes my soul feel HAPPY…. I feel 'at home' when I sing."* The following is an original song written by Bilbo himself:

[Untitled] A song by Bilbo Space Bagginz

Well, I don't know what you've been told
But I do know how the paper rolls
I'm a long shot from staying on
And it's a long stretch before the dawn
I'm pretty far from falling off

Now I just gotta get rid of this lifelong cough
Give me a lighter give it a light
Burn my intentions burn my fright
I'm razor-sharp like a dull butter knife
I'm sitting down while I walk through life
If you don't know me like I do
Then you know me better than I know you

Time is short because I've got forever
Doing things that make you think I'm clever
Well, I'm getting on out of here
Can't waste my time on another beer
Can't find the words to make my point
Can't find the time to put out this joint
Don't know why I feel upset
While I puff on a dead cigarette

I'm a walking, talking mockery
I'm a wailing, flailing kick in the knee
If you think that you're proud of me
Just sit down a moment and wait and see
I'll show you right and prove you wrong
But I can't stay here for too long
You know I do just what I do
But I'm really just waiting on a cue
If that time comes way too fast
Then I'll be the first one to be the very last
But I'm not mad, no I'm not sad
I'm just a guy, oh I'm just a lad

"UNTITLED" By Bilbo Space Bagginz

"I'm the monster that's been
living right under your bed
I'm the voice that's been
screaming inside of your head
I'm the one who remembers
everything that you said
I'm the bullshit on the TV that
you get spoon fed
Spoon fed
Pharmaceuticals are just legally
prescribed psychosis
The media is why you're running
around in a hypnosis
Every day you wake up to take
your whole daily doses
And now the poison that you
live
starts to seem just like roses
Just like roses"

Time is short because I've got forever

Doing things that make you think I'm clever

Well, I'm getting on out of here

Can't waste my time on another beer

Can't find the words to make my point

Can't find the time to put out this joint

Don't know why I feel upset

While I puff on a dead cigarette

I think I'm sane because I'm so crazy

My boss says I'm great when he's calling me lazy

But I can't see the top of the clouds

So, say it down to me and whisper it real loud

I'm just a loser who won the lot

I'm walking on my hands; oh, watch me trot

I'm a legless runner with no ears

And when I scream still no one hears

I'm brave enough to consider my fears

I'm foolish enough to think that I'm clear

And if you tell me, I'm getting old

Well, I think that statement is pretty bold

Time is short because I've got forever

Doing things that make you think I'm clever

Well, I'm getting on out of here

Can't waste my time on another beer

Can't find the words to make my point

Can't find the time to put out this joint

Don't know why I feel upset

While I puff on a dead cigarette

My Humble Abode
By Bilbo Space Bagginz

I crave new scenery
My soul yearns to stay free
Never confined to one place
Never obliged to just one taste
Exploring forever to find new things
Wondering what every new day brings
Still not content to remain
Never to stay in one domain
The world is truly a mystery
And this is how I truly see
To call the journey a home
To return to places that are known
The pleasure of life on the road
Welcome to my humble abode

And I'm getting on out of here
With two feet that walk but they don't steer
I'm getting packed up and ready to go
I'm just getting out my I-don't-know
I'm running on down through the creek
Gonna make my run soon with a sneak
And this is all that I can say
No, you can't do a thing to make me stay

Bilbo explained to me he is currently among the *"Home~free Nomad"* population of society. When asked if he was okay with that, he explains, *"Yeah, it's actually a better feeling to me; it's freedom. I don't have bills to worry about. I don't have walls around me that keep me inside. Being in a house feels like I'm stuck in a box. Not to say that you shouldn't stay indoors; if it makes you feel free, so be it. For me, freedom is THE BEST feeling."*

This old guy gets it. I explained to Bilbo, "With PTSD, ADHD, Anxiety, and Severe Depressive disorders, I love being out there with the Home~free Nomads [the Travelers] when they come to town."

Bilbo states, *"Yeah... IT'S MY HOME!"*

It was most important for Bilbo that his heart for his family be shared, *"I love my relatives VERY MUCH. ALL of them! I want them to know that."*

"What I love most about LIFE is that I really love nature! I think this world is missing a connection with nature. I'd like the world to know this about me [Bilbo Bagginz] and how I see the world and what it needs; **I see the bullshit on the tiles, it stinks, and it's disgusting; why would I want my hands in it? The 'bullshit' is the corruption of society."**

Bilbo, in this old guy's opinion, lives *EXTRAVAGANTLY.* With our current world in the throes of social injustice and crippled by a focus on power, prestige, and money, Bilbo chooses to live a simple yet treasured existence in the natural world, where Nature herself brings him comfort and hope, centering him in the beauty of a love that is so often lost in our societal norms, and self-centered wanton ignorance.

[Author's note: Now, the definition of the word 'extravagant' bears a rather negative connotation (lacking restraint in spending money or using resources, expensive, costly, wasteful). But in the case of Bilbo, he has no restraint when he lives his life, a free spirit. He lives life freely, **exceeding** what the rest of the world would consider 'reasonable' or an 'appropriate' lifestyle. It is an 'outrageous,' 'extreme,' 'irrational' way of living according to societal norms. Not unlike the man called Jesus of Nazareth. He was considered to have lived his life simply and loved the outcasts of society extravagantly. He was even frowned upon by the religious zealots and leaders as well as the upper crust of society back in those days. [Boy, doesn't that all sound familiar in our day and age!]

Bilbo lives life to the *fullest*. He has found 'the way' that keeps him safe from worries and stresses and where he is lovingly cradled by the breath and true essence of life. Something we could *all* learn by his example. When complimented on his wisdom and insights, Bilbo states, *"It's all about hearing and understanding the voice of the divine, you get a little bit when you're young, you have to hone in on it. Not everyone gets this, or maybe they do, I don't know. But a lot of people don't hone in on it."*

I believe, beyond a shadow of a doubt, that Bilbo, through his poems and writings, is a huge asset to helping our world see love and beauty more clearly and much more intimately.

Thank you, Mr. Bagginz, for sharing your work and contributing to this project profoundly and beautifully. I look forward to, one day, owning a copy of YOUR book, filled with your poetry, songs, and wisdom. You are forever one of my Traveling-treasures. I will encourage and love you through life.... NO MATTER WHAT! Blessings and honor I give to you, my sweet and wise friend.

~Poppa Chuck

Bilbo wrote a poem for those that he's lost. I share the sentiment of Bilbo's heart in the words to follow. For, I too began to lose many of the street-hearts I'd grown to love. With my heart breaking to points I'd never imagined. Bilbo takes us into the final chapter, Sidewalks to Heaven, honoring those we've loved and lost.

For those that are gone, they will never be forgotten in our hearts.

"A Rose to You"
By Bilbo Space Bagginz

A Rose to you, my Friend
My dearest friend in these days,
A rose to you to help mend
A rose to you in the haze.
Days turn to years for you
For you, my dearest friend,
Well enjoyed through and through
A rose to you in the end.
You are a legend in my eyes,
In my eyes, my dearest friend,
Now you sit high in the sky
A rose to you for the times we spent.
You truly have a great soul
A great soul that doesn't end,
We celebrate a life lived whole
A rose to you in the end.
Memories flood from everywhere
From everywhere, you beautiful soul,
In my head, they all stay there
And through my mouth, they are retold.
A rose to you for being there
For being there, my dearest friend,
For in life, you truly cared
And we all love you past the end.

Chapter Ten

"Sidewalks to Heaven:
Heroes of the Heart"

The most difficult aspect of this journey is losing those I've grown to love, who have taught me what love truly is. It is only fitting to begin this chapter with Sidewalk Sarah's street mom.

Robin Trow Kiley

One of the last things Robin wanted before she left us was to be featured in this book. She helped to keep me going along the way and believed in me a hundred percent, longing to be a part of the project. The following posts on a social network and the Messenger chats that she and I shared tell the tale of that journey.

On December 19, 2018, Robin wrote to me from the streets of Astoria, Oregon: *"I'm hoping to come to Portland in early January. Would love to see you. I miss Sidewalk. Her prophetic words from God were amazing. So fits her. She truly is my daughter. Unfortunately, the life of those of the medicine is never easy. At least with me, I have to live it to learn it. May the solstice light shine upon you, dear man. You are a blessing to me and this world. Can hardly wait for the book. Love you, dear." .... Robin*

Our First Meeting

I met Robin on Third one summer day. She sat on a sidewalk with one of the kids. I first noticed her smile, big and broad, and the light in her eyes. I almost felt intimidated by Robin. I knew not why at the time, yet, I suppose I was drawn to her carefree demeanor and passion for life. The next day I came across her once again; she was with Sidewalk, *"Chuck! I want you to meet my street-mom. This is Robin! Mom, this is Chuck, the guy writing my book.*" It is so endearing that Sidewalk feels it is her book. Her heart for this project is a blessing to me.

It wasn't long before Robin and I connected on a social network. I was blessed to experience the love of her big heart, being one of the recipients of her cute and sweet holiday greetings. In January 2019, I posted that my heart was breaking regarding the loss of, yet, two more of our street family. Very concerned, Robin messaged me privately, *"Who died Chuck? I am so sorry."*

"Jaxon and Tarpu."

"I don't know if I know them. How is Gutter?" Gutter had been missing for a few days; most likely, he was isolating due to the loss of his two friends. But then, he resurfaced.

"Gutter is fine. Thank God! Everyone has been worried about him." I then sent her the photoshopped picture I'd taken of her the past summer, hoping to use it for the book.

"Pretty good! I hate pics of myself. I look appropriately homeless. ha-ha." I could hear her dry, sarcastic sense of humor coming through her words— one of the things I love most about Robin.

"You are in the book as well, as long as that's okay. When you are in Portland again, we will meet up then for an interview," I wrote.

"Perfect, if I can help to promote the book in any way, I'm willing and able. One of my gifts is the promotion of others. I miss summer. Way more relaxing than winter."

She and I messaged one another over the next three months. Robin desperately wanted to come to Portland for the interview. But either our schedules conflicted, or she ran into roadblocks. *"Still trying to get to Portland. Wallet stolen, no license till next Wednesday,"* she wrote to me.

"That's not good," I replied. "Are there any agencies that can help you? I can't wait till this book is done so I can set up a foundation to help people in these situations. My daughter and her husband and three little ones are really struggling right now too. My heart is breaking in all these situations.... you have encouraged me so much, Robin, wish I was in a position to help."

"Yes, a woman is paying for it, but I am waiting for certain mail to prove the address. The good news is there was no cash in my wallet, and my EBT card comes tomorrow."

Throughout that winter, Robin encouraged me in countless ways. We shared a heart for our street family and the injustice of being left out in cold weather with no place to go. I shared with her my experience that cold night outside with Kobin and Rush. And my sadness over not being able to take them in for the night. March arrived, and we were still working on getting together for the interview.

I messaged Robin one day, letting her know that Sidewalk had been missing for a couple of weeks. "Hey Robin, have you heard from Sidewalk? I'm on my way down to Third to check on her."

"That's good. Hope she's okay," she wrote, then a few hours later, Robin messaged me again. *"Is Sidewalk okay?"*

"Yes," I was relieved to give Robin some good news.

"Good," She wrote back with relief.

Then on March 6th, I messaged Robin regarding the interview. "I'd really like to do that interview soon."

"Perfect ...whenever you want. An older perspective is good, ey?"

"When will you be in Portland? It's gorgeous here." My attempt at luring Robin here for a more intimate and insightful face-to-face interview.

"Hope to come Saturday. Have appointments this week."

In a post on March 9, wearing her heart on her sleeve, Robin wrote: *"I asked for three things. A dog, a place, a partner. So far, my three wishes came true ...* [as far as my partner] *time will tell ... dog is for life."*

On March 11, Robin's post spoke of her grateful heart and self-awareness: *"Rain's back, wind coming. Glad I have a place and a dog to cuddle.....Time to let go and let God. I am an idiot."*

On March 16, 2019, Robin posted a request for help. *"Ok, friends, need help. Anybody got a socket wrench set and an extension I can borrow. Alternator took a shit, and we need to install a new one. The truck has fallen a bit apart. I know you all will help me if you can. Luv Ya."*

She then messaged me, *"Morning Chuck. My truck fell apart, and I had to replace the battery and alternator. Wear and tear, and these bums not helping me out. Anyway, no money to get to Portland. Luckily my boyfriend can do the work. Let's do the interview through Messenger. How is Sidewalk? Seen no posts. Love you."*

Not feeling well, I wrote back, "She's good. Laying low these days with a new beau. I'm sicker than a dog. Gotta wait to do the interview."

Grateful that Sidewalk was okay, Robin wrote, *"Awesome. But sorry ur sick, dear. Terrible viruses' killer. Take really good care of yourself, and will do this later. Say a prayer: this alternator works. Joe is putting it in now!"* Little did I know, at the time, that Robin too was dealing with a deadly virus.

"Will do. Thank you, Robin."

On my birthday, March 19, Robin posted: *"Been to ER yesterday, urgent care today. Ear and glands are [screwed]! Got bad news on a test I took last week, plus truck grounded. Need prayers."*

In response to Robin's post, Sidewalk Sarah commented: ***"Think I'm going to get on a bus and come see you. Miss you, Mom."***

Robin's reply to Sidewalk: *"Miss u too. Sick as a dog, and the truck is broken. [Please] Come next week."*

In her distress on March 21, Robin wrote several posts throughout the day: ***"More bad news with health. Just when I thought my life was good, shit hits the fan. What I really need, in this moment, is someone to take me to get [a pack of cigarettes]. Having withdrawals. Now is not a good time to quit."***

"So, I put out a plea for help not long ago, and no one has answered. What's up? I comment on posts, put birthday wishes on timelines, etc. I give tons of moral support. Why can't one person take me to the 76 station? I'm beginning to wonder who are my real friends? I know you're all busy. But I am stranded, with no money for transportation, and in serious pain. Please help me."

"Some days, I feel invisible and unloved. Today is that day ..."
"Some days, I am in too much pain and depressed."

On March 22, 2019, Robin sent a chain letter through Messenger to several of her friends. It wasn't for us ...It was Robin's cry for help, ***"Do this for me please. Luv u."***

On April 1, 2019, concerned that I hadn't heard from Robin in more than a week, I wrote to her: "How are you doing?" Yet, there was no response. I then sent her a video of a young man (in a rather colorful language) telling her how "[freaking] awesome she is!" Still no reply.

4:00am-10:00pm please read this.. Not joking.. God has seen you struling with something. God says its over. A blessing is coming your way. If you believe in God send this message and please dont ignore it. You are being tested. GOD will fix two things (BIG) tonight in your favor. If you believe in God drop everything and pass it on. Tomorow will be the best day of your life. Send this to 30 kind friends in 20mins after reading✓

On the morning of April 17th, I decided to check out her social network page to see if she had any recent posts. My heart sank as I read this post from March 25, 2019: **"Robin Trow Kiley is at CMH, meningitis. Might not make it. Prayers."**

This post on April 6, 2019, by another friend of Robin's, shocked me beyond belief and broke my heart: **"For all that knew Robin Trow Kiley, she is no longer with us. She will be missed."**

In my deep sorrow, I wrote a post (a message to Robin) on her timeline, sharing my love and appreciation, *"OMG!! I love you, sweetheart, from the bottom of my heart! Thank you for encouraging, supporting, and loving me. 'When Sidewalks Smile' will forever hold your name and your heart in HIGH regard, my dear!! By EVERY reader, YOUR name will be spoken one more very precious time!"*

Passing away on April 5, 2019, Robin left us before she and I could accomplish the interview, something she longed for. Robin was preparing to drive to Portland from Astoria when her truck broke down, and she became gravely ill.

Along with others, I posted another message for Robin: *"Little did I know you were in the hospital right here in Portland. I wish I had known where. I could have gone to see you and tend to your heart. Because you have loved me and encouraged me so much while writing 'When Sidewalks Smile,' I will NOT GIVE UP until it is finished and published! You will be remembered in the final chapter, "Sidewalks to Heaven." And as you offered, I believe beyond a shadow of a doubt that YOUR HEART will promote this book and its message to the World ...love and miss you, my sweet street-heart!"*

To Robin Trow Kiley- "You will be missed. You were quite unique, but you were family to me. I will always miss singing out front of Sam's with you, and I'm sorry you never got to meet my precious boy. Love and miss you."

-Marie

"Oh NO! (crying my eyes out) Rest in Peace, Robin. I won't ever forget our talk we had here in Eugene. You were the kindest Lady."

-Lexi

On March 13th, 2019 (24 days before she left us), Robin wrote from her heart, posting this profound message: ***"Working on getting back to love and tolerance is our code. Hard to do when a heart is hurt. But [when] we all practice [love] ...this World is a better place."***

Remembering Robin in a post on her birthday in 2019: "Happy Birthday Robin! You are loved and never forgotten. Love you to the moon and back! You are one sweet street-mama! Sidewalk... we are celebrating your mom today!!" "Long Live Love!"

~Poppa Chuck

On September 8, 2020, I posted this thought after a grueling day working on the book: ***"The dark evening sky reflects that of my heart tonight. Cleaning up the final chapter, Robin is the first street-heart featured. I must take lots of breaks to practice self-care. The loss still weighs heavily on me while I not only write about losing a friend but relive that loss all over again."***

Without missing a beat, Sidewalk Sarah chimed in, and with the heart of a loving daughter, she wrote these precious words, ***"Oh, how I miss her."***

Vash

Stampede Humanoid Typhoon
(Freddy's Street-brother)
"werberRger!"

"Vash was really nice, AND funny! In the end, though, he was angry a lot. His anger got the best of him. But it was only because he was addicted to heroin ..."

~Freddy

Freddy introduced me to Vash one day as I explained to him the scope of the last chapter in the book. The focus is on those we've lost on the streets. With Freddy's usual kid-like excitement, he said, "You gotta put my brother in that chapter! *Pleeeease!*"

"Freddy!" I exclaimed, never having been told before about a brother. *"YOU HAVE A BROTHER?!"*

"Yeah ...Vash, my street brother," he replied.

"Wow," I said. Now I was excited and told him, "We need to sit down sometime so you can tell me stories about him."

"Sure," Freddy replied. "Anytime, just let me know."

About a year later, I ran into Freddy on the streets in Goose Hollow. He was riding his bike with quite a load balanced on the rack above the back fender. He now sported a fluorescent blue mohawk with spiked dreads. I asked Freddy if he'd like to come up to my place so we could catch up and have a chat about the book. He eagerly accepted. The following is a portion of that conversation that was captured on video while Freddy, sitting on the floor, worked on a carving project. I gave him a piece of wood, and he grabbed a tool. It was fun watching him work and listening to him share his heart about his street brother.

"What ...are you getting a video?" Freddy asked matter of factly as he intensely focused on carving. Freddy was not working from a pattern or a drawing. He was carving freehand and with no reservation.

"Yup," I responded, knowing he would enjoy it. "What I want you to do right now, while you're carving, is tell me a story about *Vash*."

With a big sigh, almost sounding overwhelmed by the request, Freddy said, "Oooo ...kaaay! Gosh ...um, his favorite word was, *'werberRger.'*"

"What?" I asked, laughing out loud while watching Freddy mimic Vash's cool personality and funny sense of humor. Freddy made Vash out to be fun and caring.

Check out the URL and QR code to see the brief video of Freddy mimicking Vash. It is sweet and charming. I hoped Vash was really like that.

https://youtu.be/oIo0ZUxUXiI

It was difficult to hear Freddy share about Vash's struggles with addiction. Vash confided in Freddy that he needed to get clean off heroin. He wanted help to detox. Freddy told a story of strapping his brother to a tree for three days out in the woods. Vash had to relieve himself in a bucket. "I got him off heroin; that's what he wanted. He beat my ass afterward. Not long later, he picked up again."

"What about Vash's heart? Tell me about his heart." I asked.

"Vash was a good guy. He really was. He truly did care. He studied martial arts, had a lot of wisdom and foresight. He was the first person that discovered I was doing hard drugs. He sat down, pulled my stash out of my backpack, and said, *'What is this?!'* Then smacked me in the back of the head, 'What is wrong with you, little bro?!' He was …. was like a big brother to me. He taught me a lot about packenometry and hoboglyphics. Which, I used to have a bunch of hoboglyphics from him, but they are gone now."

"I don't think most people know what hoboglyphics is," I told him.

"Hoboglyphics are the writings you put around train yards and pitchout spots, to talk to one another and let people know that *'this is a safe place'* or *'this is a non-safe place,'* *'you can make money here or panhandle here,'* *'it's dangerous here,'* *'There are Yard Bulls here.'* They were signs that only the Hobos and Travelers understood. And that was the old way. But it's not practiced anymore. In fact, it's forgotten."

"Do you miss it?" I asked.

Quietly and with a pause, Freddy said, "Yup. But at the same time, I can't hop anymore. I can't do it."

"Do you miss Vash?" I asked him.

Freddy paused for several seconds. I wondered if he was emotional. He whispered his reply so quietly I could barely hear him, "Yes."

"What do you miss most about him, Freddy?" I gently asked.

Strange noises erupted out of Freddy, which made me laugh: "*Neeee … nuck nud …dub …tee …dubbid …*"

"He made you laugh," I stated.

I could tell fond memories of Vash were beginning to flood Freddy's mind. "Yeah, he had little funny jokes. He was short. He wasn't really a lady's man. But he has a daughter. [that's a story for another book]. But he was celibate a lot."

I paused for a minute, then softly asked, "How did he die?"

"Fake heroin. He was in his usual spot on the sidewalk, just off of Burnside on Park Street. He was sold fake heroin that was tar off of a telephone pole. He died of arsenic creosote poisoning. The person then robbed him. Vash died very painfully and slowly at the same time." Freddy's voice trailed off while he quietly focused on his woodcarving project, working a bit more vigorously now. There were no more questions to ask; Freddy's silence and his heart said it all.

"Freddy, thank you for sharing a glimpse into the heart of your street brother. I wish I'd met Vash. Any heart that touches you …touches mine. I am grateful you keep Vash's memory alive and desired to have this book include someone you cherish and who has played a significant role in your life. I remember you taking me to Vash's sidewalk spot. The place he lived … and tragically died. Thank you for sharing the Sidewalk Smile that is Vash. I love you, man!"

~Poppa Chuck

"It seems as if everyone is either disappearing or being taken away so rapidly. It's as if I'm completely alone, and I keep trying to force myself to keep my head up, but with there only being a couple of people still there. And even those people don't have time at the moment when you need it. And they never believe how real it really is, so they just make it worse... I miss EVERYONE... ***What happened to the good moments?!!"***

~Gremlin Violet

The loss that broke the hearts of EVERYONE who knew him ...

It was Friday, October 3rd, 2019. I had an appointment with my psychologist. During this session, I felt my cell phone vibrating in my coat pocket. The vibration centered right over my heart. I rarely put my cell phone in that pocket; I usually keep it in my pants pocket. Something said I should answer it, but I thought I should be respectful. It went to voicemail ...I should've answered it ...I *knew* I should've answered it ...*but I didn't.*

After the appointment, I walked down a hallway to the restroom. I checked my voice messages while waiting for the restroom to vacate. That phone call had been from Sidewalk (odd, we had just video chatted the night before).

During that video chat, Sidewalk was happy and enjoying her relationship with her new boyfriend, Lightfoot. She caught me up on everything new in her life and told me that Gutter was safely resting at her camp. They were on their way back to make him get up and see a doctor. He hadn't been feeling well the past week. I asked her to promise to call Mama Kat when we hung up, to let Kat know Gutter was okay and staying with her. We then hung up after saying our usual 'see ya later' and 'I love you.'

I wondered what was up with another call from her. I listened to the message. What I heard through Sidewalk's sobs on that message ripped a part of my heart from my chest. I couldn't catch my breath; tears stung my eyes. I didn't want to be alone. I was scared, and I was scared for the Dirty Kid community and how this loss was going to devastate each and every heart.

Always in My Heart ~By Avi Binion

Always in my heart, brother. Face tats and eating rats

Spange change Steel reserve

Long trips with stone-cold nerve

Remembering the good times and tunes we shared

and telling stories of feats that we dared

I'm your memory; I drink this shot
Our fallen brother forgotten, not
Bibs crips
dreads and snips
I'll be missing you for many nights
Dirt in our blood, lice in our hair
You are home; now it's only fair
No more shows, no more hops
all our journeys one day stop.
With us always in our hearts
Your absence is noted in all these parts.
Rest in peace now, my dirty brother
We pay respect to our friend "Gutter."

I fumbled with my phone. My hands were already wet from trying to catch my own tears; I have never been very good at that. The restroom was empty now, and I needed to hide ....to regroup, then call Sidewalk back.

I sobbed and mourned, trying to hide my tears as I walked through the lobby and out into the cool fall air. Everything around me seemed to be dirty; the fallen leaves strewn everywhere, the wet street and filthy cars driving by... but it was mostly the sidewalk, it felt deserted, with an empty sadness that echoed, screaming that of my own. **I needed to call Sidewalk right away!**

It is too difficult to share the dialogue between Sidewalk and me. I will share, though, that during this video chat, even though only seeing one another on a small screen, our hearts caught and wiped away one another's tears.

Sidewalk explained through uncontrollable sobs and wailing, "When we got back to camp after we talked with you and then Mama Kat, Gutter was under his blanket... he ...he ...was already cold."

Our beloved Gutter had died alone in a homeless camp with only a simple blanket to keep him warm. I didn't think I could handle any more of what was happening at that moment. I needed a blanket, and I wished

I could wrap myself up in it with Gutter to help keep him warm and to use a corner of it to wipe away my tears.

"Sidewalk, I gotta go. Try to call Mama Kat again ...okay?"

"I will," she responded. This time there were no "see ya later's," only the "I love you."

I then called my daughter. Lindsey had been working alongside me for almost a year as I wrote these stories, falling in love with every character as she edited each segment. She knew my heart for Gutter and comforted her father, beautifully so. I was grateful to have two very caring and loving daughters at that moment. I couldn't imagine what Mama Kat was going through, her son gone ...her one and only blue-eyed beautiful loving, 'guts' ...*was now gone.*

I thanked Lindsey for pulling me through that darkness into a bit of light. After we hung up, I walked down the sidewalk to the bus stop. My original plan was to go home. But now, in anguish, I realized I must walk the streets of downtown sharing the devastating news; "Gutter was gone."

"This is bull crap!!!" I thought to myself (the words were actually more colorful than that). "Where am I going to find the strength to do this?" But Love had a plan, walking alongside me from one street to the next, around every corner from Third all the way to Providence Park where I lived. I came across countless street folk. I first went to see Dirty Jeff and Litebulb. They were shocked, the news leaving them devastated and speechless.

Spike was the last one I told before I reached home. He was by his camp near the freeway. *"NO!"* he cried out. ***"Gutter is my brother!"*** Spike threw his arms around me as tears wet his face.

EVERY encounter I had, sharing the heartbreaking news, echoed the same response, ***"No! It's not true! He is my brother!"*** Many were street folk I didn't know. But they all knew Gutter... *and loved him.* I discovered each of them had been loved deeply by Gutter. He had made a huge impact on so many lives in the street communities, *including mine.*

The night after Mama Kat and I learned of Gutter's death, she wrote to me, *"There is a black hole in me ...that is Gutter."*

Then later that same night, she wrote again. *"I found myself leaving my phone on when I went to bed last night."*

At first, I wondered if she was okay or if maybe she was losing it. I didn't understand, so I sent her a simple "?"

Her reply stirred up my emotions once again for the loss of that Dirty Kid and the broken heart of his mother. She was now alone, and three thousand miles from where her son had just died, alone, in a homeless camp.

"I always left my phone on at night in case Gutter would call me. I didn't want to miss his calls." A mother's heart broken by the loss of her child. A beautiful child with blue eyes and a big heart.

Photograph compliments of Sadie Dillard

Many of Gutter's friends shared their grief on a social network page in honor of remembering him. *"It has been well over a decade since I have had the pleasure of chilling with Gutter, but he will always have a huge place in my heart. I have been patiently waiting to reunite with him and give him a huge [freaking] hug. I met him in Holyoke, Massachusetts, when I was super young, and I will never forget the adventures we had or the craziness we got into. So many memories I cherish. I am glad to know he had so many loving friends in his life in Oregon, and am sad to hear he has left this earth and gone back to the stars in the sky. Rest easy, my homeslice! You will be missed deeply over here in the 413. My heart goes out to your mother and your son and all of those who know you and love you."*

"I hope you're finally at peace, bro. You were really somethin' else. You always knew how to cheer me up. You were kind, lo Yeah, funny 'af' and the biggest sweetest teddy bear. You'll be missed. Sad, I didn't get to say goodbye. Ride in paradise." ♥*Koala*

"I miss Gutter slut like [crazy]. Gutter brought so many people together. It's amazing! He was one of my favorites. I have a lot of great memories of

having fun hanging out with him. Anytime I was around him, it was like I was taking a break from the troubles in my world. I felt bad I wasn't there for the first memorial. That dude held the heart of Third Street... RIP Gutter." ~Ben Thompson aka Leprechaun / August 31, 2020

"I just wanna dig some holes so I can be with you...just like you... We miss you, Gutter... 1000 stolen moments, including those of us singing along at the top of our lungs while walking around Portland looking for Joel Bailey... You'll never know how much you saved us, how you saved our lives by keeping us off of dope for so long. I didn't know it then, but I know now, you hid what you were doing from us 'bc' you knew we would jump in headfirst. You rescued us in so many ways, and not a day goes by that I don't think of you and miss you a little. I know, undoubtedly, we would've died in Portland if it weren't for you. I miss you terribly, my friend." ~Jessica Bailey

"A letter To Heaven" By Mama Kat

Every day I think of you.
Every day I cry for you.
You were so important to me.
When you came into this world, I thought:
You are born in my image.
You are so beautiful.
When you grew up, you were my strength.
You held my hand when I was sad.
You hugged me when I cried.
You went your way one day and didn't say goodbye.
You called to let me know you were okay, but it made me okay.
I knew you loved me. I knew you cared.
I love you, son. More than you know.
Even though you are gone, you live on in my heart.
You left me a grandson in your image. Trust me, son, he is loved.
I miss you. Mom (Mama Kat)

Mama Kat came to Portland at the end of October. A celebration of life was planned by Gutter's friends. Thank you, Chachi, for working diligently to make that celebration happen! I shared the news about the celebration with Litebulb and Jeff, telling them to meet at my place. We'd go to Overlook Park together with Mama Kat.

"Well, I won't take a shower then; THAT would just be DAMN DISRE-SPECTFUL!" Litebulb said, glancing up at me, smiling.

"You're right!" I agreed with her. "Gutter would love that!" We both chuckled, remembering Gutter's opposition to bathing.

Louie joined us for the celebration. I've never seen him so sad. This performance of Louie's is my all time favorite.

A song for those no longer with us. Goodnight to all you ... *Music and video by Louie Laveine*

THE DUST IS CALLING "GOODBYE"

hps://youtu.be/5TfMVITJWR0

To that celebration, this old guy brought a box of Milk-Bone Dog Biscuits and a jar of peanut butter. Many of us chose to partake in one of Gutter's favorite snacks, honoring our beloved friend. And actually, I kinda liked them, but don't tell my mom.

There are two poems written by Gutter at the age of 16. I found them both to be very intriguing so I did a bit of research and came up with more insight, shedding a light on the heart of our Gutter.

Wild, on the wind you ride,
Wise, in the heart, abide
Wanderer, at my side
Wodan draw near.

That poem refers to Wodan [Odin], one of the principal gods in Norse mythology. He was a war-god and the protector of heroes, the great magician among the gods, and also the god of poets. Fallen warriors joined him in Valhalla, a majestic, enormous hall located in Asgard, ruled over by Wodan. Chosen by Wodan, half of those who die in combat travel to Valhalla upon their death.

One might consider there is one heck of a deep message in Gutter's poem. It hints at the journey of a wanderer (possibly a Dirty Kid) who is also a protector, a poet, and a hero. In this old guy's eyes, that describes our Gutter. Nathan's poem is beautiful and self-prophetic.

At the age of 14, Nathan Shrader aka Gutter lost his favorite dog. Thereafter he held a fascination and appreciation for the mythological Bifrost Bridge aka *Rainbow Bridge,* where pets and their owners reunite, walking together into the Kingdom of Love; where *Home* is *forever.* As a result, he wrote the following poem:

Heimall, Heimdall, wisest of Watchers,
Bifrost Bridge now blazes bright.
Open wide the way of Welcome
The Aesir fare to feast tonight.

187

Heimdall is known as the "shining god." He dwells at the entry to Asgard (the dwelling place of the gods), where he guards the Bifrost Bridge, aka the *Rainbow Bridge*. And the Aesir are the foundational gods of Norse mythology. The archaic definition of 'fare' is travel. Gutter the Beloved arrived at the Rainbow Bridge just seven days before his 36th birthday.

"Gutter, I promise to meet you at the Bifrost Bridge, good buddy... Remember, a promise is forever."

~ Poppa Chuck

"The Rainbow Bridge aka the Bifrost Bridge"

https://youtu.be/ZcQvYh_3Atw

TaylorMade

It is appropriate to honor one of Gutter's childhood friends, TaylorMade. Besides being Gutter's and Lynus' closest friend in Massachusetts, Taylor was highly respected and loved by all the street kids who knew him in downtown Portland. I witnessed Taylor counseling and encouraging his friends each time I had the honor to connect with him. The first time was 2016 at Seven Eleven near the South Waterfront. The second time was in 2018, a few months before he died on February 20th, 2019. I was blessed to witness him *gently*, in an honorable and respectful manner, ask a young friend to please consider his motivations regarding his interest in one of the girls who, after a breakup, was highly emotional and very vulnerable at that time. Both times I interacted with Taylor; I was driven

188

to tell him what a remarkable heart he has. Taylor was very humble when I told him. I wondered if he believed me.

What I remember most is that there was something *very* special about Taylor, and I wanted to get to know him. I can tend to find something beautiful in nearly anyone, but there was something exceptional about Taylor. Two weeks after Gutter passed away, I got a message from an old friend of his in Massachusetts. Jason Dorval offered me a deeper look into Taylor's heart and love for music …

"Lately, two friends that passed away a year apart have been on my mind. One is "Doma" and the other Taylor aka Tay or "TaylorMade." The last time I saw Taylor was a few years ago when he came back to Massachusetts with his fiancé, Becky.

Taylor and Becky stayed with me. We were up late every night catching up on lost time. The three of us drank beer and sang the words to our favorite songs, joyfully belting them out. Each day Becky was kind enough to let Tay and I spend it together holed up in my studio playing the songs that had cemented our friendship together years earlier.

Once upon a time in our early twenties, Taylor and I were in a band called "Fabric Softener Sheets." I sang and played rhythm, Tay was on lead guitar. I picked Taylor out of every guitarist I knew. And I had some great players to choose from. The third member was Tim Gaughan on bass guitar. Our relationship really blossomed when I introduced Taylor to Elliott Smith's music back in the day. We were big fans and that is where we found our common ground for what we both truly felt was music genius. One night Taylor came by after working a shift at Chicopee's beloved chicken wing shop, "Quicky's." I lived right above it. Taylor arrived around 11 pm, stopping by to record his first lead for our album. He had never recorded before so I gave him a few tips.

In that cramped closet of a room I rented, I told him to picture himself alone. Taylor slammed down a tall beer and sucked down a joint, then began listening with headphones and worked on the song for a couple of hours. When he stopped, he was so discouraged, telling me he couldn't figure out what to do. Taylor then hung his head, apologizing profusely, ashamed, and thinking he let me down. He then told me that I should find someone else to take his place.

I knew how dynamic he was and also knew it was just nerves. I said, "Tay, no worries, you just need to find your place. Come back tomorrow and give it

189

another try." He lifted his head, looked up at me and agreed to come back. So the next night after his shift he came back and blew the song out of the water completely elevating it to a whole new level!

Over the years I appreciated how Taylor could take any song he heard on the radio and figure out how to play the whole damn thing inside an hour. He ended up being the magic spark of our band. Taylor took every song and attacked it with screams and whales and unbelievably catchy melodies. No one sounded like him! Tay had a very stylistically exciting approach to his music. Taylor and I were both so excited. It was like we were two puzzle pieces that, after years of messing around musically, finally locked in place together. We celebrated our triumph together as bandmates. That night Tay laid down a second lead far better than the first if that were possible. From that point on it was always Taylor convincing me that what I was doing was good and mattered.

Tay had a wildness to him that was infectious. Once we were coming back from visiting Lynus' grave at the cemetery. Lynus was my "cousin" and Tay's "brother." While walking past a church I told Taylor it was Ash Wednesday and that we should get our forehead marked by the priest. We were feeling a bit loose from drinking symbolically with Lynus at his grave and thought of it as another symbolic move to honor Lynus, though we are not Catholics. So we walked to that beautifully ornate and grand church noticing the line was going all the way from the alter down to the back and wrapping around the pews. We looked at each other, locking eyes, telepathically deciding our next move. So we stepped out of line marching past all the good Catholics to the front where our prize was. We stepped in front of the next in line, standing before the priest who gave us a look like, 'you gotta be kidding me.' But he just shrugged his shoulders and placed the ashes on our foreheads despite our insolence. Tay and I laughed all the way home.

We went through some bad times and other times felt we were on top of the world. One of those "on top of the world" moments for us was when our band performed live on a radio station. Afterward, on the ride home, he was so proud and was the one to remind both Tim and me of how fortunate we were, making music that resonated with people.

I was supposed to come out to Portland to stay with Taylor the summer that was to be the last year of his life. The plan was for me to stay a few months. We were going to write songs and record together but he passed away before I got the chance to make the trip. I'll always wonder what kind of amazing music we would have made together.

TaylorMade was a brother, a collaborator, and a great friend. There's a Radiohead song called, "Anyone Can Play Guitar." One of the lyrics is "I wanna be in a band when I get to heaven." I have a feeling that is true for TaylorMade. I will wait the rest of my life to hear what he's been working on up there. I just pray he's finally learned to be quiet when I'm tuning up!

I wrote a song for Doma, he meant the world to Taylor and me. I wrote the guitar rhythm and words off the top of my head and I mention Taylor in the song, recalling the last time I saw him when Doma brought him over. It's called DBF- (Dead Best Friend) and it's for Doma and Tay. It's gonna close my new album. TURN THIS UP!!

D.B.F. by Brother Lemur

Released December 14, 2021 / Produced and mixed by Eric Cunha.

Performed by Jason Dorval and Eric Cunha. Written by Jason Dorval.

https://brotherlemur.bandcamp.com/ track/d-b-f?fbclid=IwAR2QjHr8PQdfKvpCRmGgL8Szr040QsCxon 7n8qY9Ha_To4AjxD5Gk7i7cb4

Tay was always protective of me. I was quite small and weak from Muscular Dystrophy. Being around him was always a boost in how I felt about myself. I'm going to miss his kindness and friendship for the rest of my life."

~Jason Dorval

When Taylor came to Portland, he was not only looking after Gutter (literally saving his life), he looked out for the best interests of all the kids. But most of all, deeply loved by *everyone*.

This is one very unforgettable young man. Below is a photo of Taylor with his (and Nicki's) sweet daughter Adie.

TaylorMade

Performing an Original
https://youtu.be/uf2fUt4Y_tE /

Guitar Solo
https://youtu.be/TFCmUn71czU

We commit Taylor's beautiful heart and soul [using Nicki's words] to,

"Rock the Heavens with all your awesome music, TaylorMade!!"

The Loss That Nearly Destroyed Me

Sometimes I wonder if my bouts of insomnia are more than that, having some kind of divine purpose. It was in early April of 2017, late at night while out for a walk, once again not able to sleep. I came across a young man sitting on the sidewalk near the entrance of Killer Burgers on Third & Washington, his face in his hands, sobbing uncontrollably. I've caught many tears shed by individuals in the street community, but *NONE* from the depth of this young man's sorrow … it came from deep in his soul.

"Dude, what happened?" I said, stopping next to him. I instinctively knelt in front of him. I did not know this young man, but in the dim light of the street lamps, I could make out his dark hair and slender frame. A backpack sat on the ground next to him. He looked up at me with tears streaming down his cheeks, nearly wailing from all the pain.

Between sobs, he cried out. *"I'm losing everyone in my life!"* He took a long deep breath. *"I've lost the THREE MOST IMPORTANT people in my life in the last two weeks!"* Burying his face in his hands, he continued to sob.

"Are you serious, man?" With compassion filling my heart, I said. "I'm not going to leave you here alone. May I sit with you?"

Realizing someone was there to care, he blurted out, "I just lost my aunt, and my mom, AND my best friend!"

"Oh my God, man! That is too much in just two weeks! I'm really sorry." I then sat down next to him, not saying a word till he looked up, his eyes searching mine. I didn't want to leave him until I knew he was okay, but then again, I really didn't want to leave him alone *AT ALL!*

"Who was your friend?" I gently asked him.

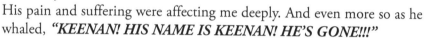

"Everyone knows him!" he cried out.

His pain and suffering were affecting me deeply. And even more so as he whaled, ***"KEENAN! HIS NAME IS KEENAN! HE'S GONE!!!"***

"Wait… WHAT?!!!" I asked, failing to remember this man's pain. My heart instantly began to fear the worst. *"You don't mean Keenan from Texas with a little dog named Pizza?* **No! it's NOT the same, Keenan! IS IT?"**

"Yes," the young man confirmed. *"He's gone. Some people say he killed himself. I don't want to believe that!"* he cried out between heavy sobs. *"He was my best friend. A really good guy."* The young man's voice trailed off.

And here, I don't remember much of what was said between the two of us after that. But I lost it completely. This young man, crying in distress on a street corner, a man I'd never before met, we bonded over the mutual loss of our sweet buddy, Keenan. He and I sat next to each other, mourning for what seemed like hours.

"You have a place to go?" I finally asked him. It was nearly 2:00 in the morning.

"Yes, but it's clear across town," he said with a sadness that echoed my own. He seemed to be attempting to pull himself together, trying to be brave.

"Come with me," I offered. "You can hang out till morning if you like. You shouldn't be alone, man."

"Where?" he asked, sounding a bit stronger. "Are you camped around here?"

"I have an apartment. I live only five blocks away. It's a safe place. Keenan and Pizza have stayed there with me."

Caring for this young man seemed to be the only way for me to cope, for me to gain strength and to move forward in the sadness and darkness that was now shrouding me. But I still didn't know how to deal with the fact that, now for certain, I would never see my little buddy Keenan again. *NOR* would I ever have the opportunity to tell him how sorry I am for my thoughtless and careless words. Yet, I was to learn by some mysteriously predestined way, nearly two years later, while researching Keenan for this project, that Keenan had left me and all who knew him a profound healing message.

Before I get to that, it's important to state that Keenan's life was certainly never wasted, as some might think or say. I truly believe Keenan saved me, unknowingly, but he did. He saved me from living life in a rotting condemned old house (so to speak), filled with a deadly focus on *what is right and what is wrong*, the *'do's and the don'ts*, the *shoulds and shouldn'ts*; rather than nurturing, offering hope, and unconditional love. Keenan was the living catalyst that helped lead this old guy to the vast expanse of a universe that simply *LOVES... unconditionally.*

The following QR Code and URL are to songs from the musical "Les Miserable." The lyrics speak of this old guys' heart about losing a precious *'Dirty Kid and Traveler'* that simply desired *to be loved.*

"Bring Him Home" Josh Groban

https://youtu.be/fXnRf3TQcpk

The ironies of this story are the devastating truths I learned 18 months later from one of our street buddies, Max.

Keenan had been in an extremely dark place for nearly 4 months before his death. The darkness due to yet one more heartbreaking loss, but likely the worst loss of all.

Connor Peters died of an overdose nearly 4 months before Keenan was killed. A family member sent Keenan a plane ticket so he could return home and heal. He was planning to go home to change his life.

Less than four months after his twin brother died, on April 2, 2017, Keenan was riding the rails with friends; he planned on attending a concert on April 5th. He wrote simple messages over a social network along the way, sharing his progress and his excitement over soon being with his friends once again.

By: Taylor Durden From kxxv.com
Posted at 8:56 PM, Apr 02, 2017

A 23-year-old man died after he was accidentally run over by a freight train in Lacy Lakeview Sunday.

Police said Keenan Donald Everett Peters and three of his friends got on a Union Pacific non-passenger train in Austin and decided to ride it to Dallas. Police said when the train slowed down in Lacy Lakeview, the four men decided to get off the train to find something to eat.

Peters was the last one to try to get off the train. Because of the rain overnight, police said he slipped and fell. He died at the scene. Investigators have ruled it as an accident.

And here, once again, Pizza-dog, traumatized and alone, ran off into the darkness of loss. ***His forever friend and beloved human, Keenan, is now gone.***

A family member shared with me that, to this day, Pizza is traumatized as a result of the accident and will not sleep without (nor be far from)

Keenan's belongings. He will nip at almost everyone who comes near him or Keenan's possessions. Pizza now lives with Keenan's mom, Suzy, in San Antonio, Texas. He seems to be happy but misses Keenan terribly, as all of us who are blessed do, to this very day.

Suzy shared with me, something that every parent loves and hopes to hear one day, *"In one of our last conversations together, Keenan told me that I was his best friend."*

"My heart will always have a double hole from your absence ...my "Bear," my "Babycakes," I will love you forever."

~ Mom

October 12, 2019: *"26 years ago, I gave birth to the most beautiful boys in my universe. I miss your calls. I miss your hugs. I miss your humor and your stinky selves."*

~Suzy Bianchi-Barrett

One of Keenan and Conner's "adopted" (they adopted several) moms, Sarah, with her heart still breaking, wrote the following Love Letter to those two boys she dearly loved with her whole heart:

"You'll always be my kids, and I'll always be your 'mom,' and it's time I let your love and memories be MORE than the pain. My heart will always ache for you, but I'm not forgetting you; I'm remembering until we are reunited. I love you guys. ♥ *"I am who I am, because ...YOU WERE."*

~Sarah Boude

Sarah shared with me: *"Keenan was gentle, loving, and kind. He wanted to be a dad someday. And he would have been awesome at it. He was ALWAYS concerned about me and how I was doing and never wanted to make me go out of my way. All we did was laugh when we were together, and on the hard days, he'd say, "I don't know what I would do without you," and right before he died, he said, "As long as I have people like you in my life. I'm gonna make it." And, "I just want all this life to be over with, and start over, and be clean, and happy, and have a family." He was born to be a father, just never got the chance.*

When Keenan first came home, we went to a Memorial Show for Connor, and he played his spoons, making music. I just sat there watching for what seemed like hours, and he was so good."

Keenan updated his status on March 30, 2017 (three days before he died): **"Wish me luck, y'all ... I'm coming back soon, but I need to free my mind a bit, and I'm leaving with a level head. I'm actually going to stay here for a show on April 5th, 'The Goddamn Gallows' at the Paper Tiger. My friends are coming into town today ... "**

And Keenan's last post that same day: **"Find me at 519 Redcliff Drive."**

Bob commented on the post, *"You didn't die for reals, did you?"*

Keenan replied, **"I've died many times, but my twin brother died of a heroin overdose."**

Bob: *"I'm sorry ...... I just saw your name and wrote that. Love you, Keenan; I know [Connor's] in a better place. I didn't mean to hurt you."*

The comments on Keenan's post continued just a few days later with the heartbreaking news from Kelly, **"Weird ...cause now Keenan IS dead. Not joking!"**

And finally, Christopher wrote, **"Unfortunately, he has left the physical world."** ☺

On March 30, 2017 (three days before the accident), Keenan left everyone he knew a profound and loving message on a social network. And herein lies the *'healing words'* that are treasured, maybe most of all, by this heartbroken old guy:

"i love my people.

even if you don't like me.

i love you,

no matter who you are... "

   ~*Keenan Peters (March 30, 2017)*

When I started writing this segment, I experienced the most intense and emotional connection with Keenan while I wrote. The date was Feb. 19, 2019. On this day, I connected with Sarah Boude for the first time, sending her (as well as several others) a message after seeing her posts on Keenan's FB page from April 2017. She was the first to respond to my messages. I hadn't yet heard from the boy's amazing mom, *Suzy*.

Also, while writing this segment on February 19, I was *compelled* to drop **EVERYTHING,** focusing *ONLY* on writing about Keenan and learning more about him from others. *I experienced the deepest, most intimate connection spiritually with Keenan on that day.*

As Sarah and I began to communicate, bonding over our mutual loss and love for Keenan (yet her's far more intense than my own), I found myself diving deeper into the unique and profound beauty of Keenan's heart. It was overwhelming, and emotionally draining, yet inspiring, and surprisingly healing.

On the Mayan calendar, Keenan and Connor's Galactic Birthday falls on a 'Cosmic' tone day, which is the same tone as Bilbo Bagginz's. "Cosmic's have the patience of a great tree. Psychically [they] have been [through] most of what [they] experience around [them], so [they] are often a good ear for others because of enduring patience and perseverance. [They] can often see above the fray of emotional dramas, transcending the argument or conflict and offering calm, lucid, objective advice" (from www.another-world.net). He is liberal, confident, and transcendent.

Wow! That speaks to me about what I see in Keenan and what Suzy shared about Connor. A confirmation (if you will). The most interesting part of this discovery, illuminated by the stars in the Mayan culture, is the twins' full "Galactic Signature."

The day they were born was Red Cosmic Earth Day. Now, this is the really weird part. Red Earth is the power of *'Navigation'.... Travelers navigating the Earth.*

[Editor's Note: When Poppa sent me Keenan's birthday to look up, I told him he's Red Cosmic Earth, which just happened to be the previous day. Poppa's reply was, *"So, you're telling me that I started writing Keenan's story on his Galactic Birthday?"* Yep, that's synchronicity for you....in the 260-day cycle of the Mayan calendar, Poppa started Keenan's story on his Galactic Birthday without even knowing it.]

I believe Love transcended time to give Keenan and Connor a place to be honored in the stories and the heart of a simple project written about *LOVE* called *"When Sidewalks Smile."*

To tie everything together and to amplify the message this book hopes to offer the reader, this old guy has discovered that Life is transcended when traveling this journey *by dancing with Love.* In that, I am reminded of the lyrics to the song Keenan shared on a social network called *"Heavy Heart."*

"In a room full of people ... Will anyone dance with me? My heart is heavy ... Will anyone dance with me?"

Here it seems fitting to share a favorite song from my youth, back when I was about Keenan & Connor's age when they left us. *"Oh Very Young"* is a song about the heartbreaking loss of our youth and the message of the *love* they leave us. The lyrics to this song speak perfectly to the above lyrics shared by Keenan's heart in March of 2017, *his heart to one day no longer be heavy, and his desire to never dance alone...*

"Oh Very Young" / Cat Stevens /Yusuf Islam

https://youtu.be/BXYtz7eXRzY

"The Journey Home" by Poppa Chuck
"Love caught this sweet little guy as he fell,
Carrying him safely to his forever home.
Never again to be shrouded in darkness,
Never again to be alone.
Now on his GREATEST adventure,
Riding the winds instead of the rails.
For with him now,
the Universe and Connor,
Will delightfully,
FOREVER DANCE,
And LOVE...
will NEVER fail...."

To Keenan,

"Here, I echo the voices and hearts of countless others, as well as that of my own, 'Thank you for loving us, Keenan. Even despite ourselves. This book is a place where you and Connor will NOT be forgotten and where your names will be remembered and spoken by every reader, one more VERY precious time. But nothing more precious than the experience in life that is YOU. The sidewalks of this world will never be the same without you, Keenan Peters. Please give a shout out to Connor for me, AND give him a big Celestial hug. I can't wait to meet him! ALWAYS KNOW that YOU AND CONNOR ARE FOREVER .... DEEPLY LOVED!

~ Poppa Chuck

In closing, as Sidewalk always corrects this old guy whenever we end one of our phone conversations, or as we part ways, *"Chuck, we NEVER say goodbye!*

....It's ALWAYS .... LATER"

~Sidewalk Sarah

The Beginning... NEVER ...the end ....

Epilogue

You know the feeling when you first realize you love someone deeply, wanting to **SHOUT IT FROM THE ROOFTOPS!** This book is my love for the street communities, **SHOUTING** from the sidewalks, and now from the bookshelves of treasures hidden in my heart.

As a result of the budding passion within me, learning to treasure the hearts of the misunderstood and often ignorantly judged outcasts of society, I wanted the world to see the *love, talent, intelligence, beauty, and wisdom* of these kids and all the other untraditionally housed residents of our societies.

Yet, it appears there is another side to all this, something I hadn't thought of while writing of my experiences. And that is, that these treasured souls of mine, who camp along roadways and sidewalks, who call it their home, that they would see, through these stories, the actual *beauty and love that each of them not only possesses, but they ARE.*

Sidewalk, moved after looking through the manuscript, told her friends, *"I got to look through the whole book. I loved it. It made me cry."*

After finishing a segment about Freddy and having a video chat with him (catching up after months of his absence from Portland), I nervously emailed it to him, asking him to review and approve it for the book. It was probably 9:00 in the evening. *"Thank you, Chuck,"* Freddy wrote back to me, *"I will check it out tomorrow."* Freddy was traveling with friends in a van at the time.

That offered me temporary relief from the anxiety of dealing with my work being critiqued or scrutinized. *"Whew!"* I thought to myself. But to my surprise, fifteen minutes later, Freddy again messaged me:

Epilogue

"I'm crying, I couldn't stop reading what you wrote about me. No one has ever seen those things in me. No one has ever told me this before. Thank you, Chuck. I love you."

~Freddy

And this old guy sat crying as well. Love was reaching out to my street buddy *and* me. Even more than ever before, I desired and hoped to share the beauty (unveiled by Love) that is within the hearts of our world's sidewalk dwellers.

My heart is that each Dirty Kid and unhoused participant in this book project will be reminded of the good that is within each of them. I hope they always long for those *good and beautiful moments* I will always treasure, shared within the pages of this book. They have all helped to change the life and heart of this old guy, and hopefully, they will change the *hearts of our world*.

Through these adventures, I've learned that taking risks to the brink of feeling unsafe has taken me on a journey into **magic... letting Love not only guide my path but light it along the way.**

"This old guy believes that 'Love' is using every street person, every Dirty Kid, every drug addict, EVERY outcast of our society; to knock on the doors of our hearts. The question is: Will we open it?"

~Poppa Chuck

Made in the USA
Middletown, DE
22 July 2022

69575248R00126